ALAN NORU

SENIORS GUIDE
TO
 Windows 11

BONUS CHAT GPT BOOK!

Non-Tech-Savvy Step-by-Step Guide to Learn and Master All Features with Easy | Fully Large Illustrated Guide | Tailored for Seniors

- Troublesshooting
- Tips and tricks
- Large view
- Settings
- Windows update

TAILORED FOR SENIORS

TABLE OF CONTENTS

TABLE OF CONTENTS

CHAPTER 3:

Accessibility (Important for Senior Users)...68

CHAPTER 4:

Getting to Know Your Desktop......74

CHAPTER 5:

How to Setup Applications 82

CHAPTER 6:

Backup and Restore: Keep Your Memories and Documents Safe (Photos, Videos, Documents) 91

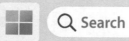

TABLE OF CONTENTS

CHAPTER 11:

Applications for Your Daily Life....141

CHAPTER 12:

Having a Good Time with Windows 11............................. 157

CHAPTER 13:

Taking Photographs and Other Activities... 169

BONUS CHAPTER 14:

BONUS CHAPTER 15:

GET YOUR FREE BOOK BONUSES NOW!

(DOWNLOAD FOR FREE WITH THE BELOW INSTRUCTION!)

Do you want to unlock the full knowledge about your fantastic Windows 11 Guide?

1) BONUS: CHAT GPT BOOK - Master Chat GPT from Scratch. The Artificial Intelligence (AI) will not be a secret for you!

SCAN THE QR CODE BELOW AND UNLOCK THE FULL POTENTIAL OF CHAT GPT!

INSTRUCTION ON HOW TO UNLOCK YOUR FREE BONUSES

Only 2 simple steps to unlock your free bonuses:

1) **Scan the QR code** on the previous page

2) **Let me know how you are excited about all the contents!**
I look forward to your opinion on the book and the bonus content!

SCAN THE QR CODE BELOW OR LEAVE A QUICK REVIEW ON THE AMAZON PRODUCT PAGE TO SHARE YOUR THOUGHTS ON THIS BOOK.

The best way to do it? Simple! **You can upload a brief video** with your thoughts. I will greatly appreciate an honest opinion about the book!

Don't you want to create a video? Don't worry! **You can do a short review with some photos** of dishes made thanks to this book or take photos of the most beautiful parts of the book.

Scan QR Code to Leave a Review Quickly!

NOTE: You don't have to feel obligated, but it would be highly appreciated!

Glossary

It's easy to be perplexed by jargon and acronyms that seem foreign in today's tech-driven world. If you've ever been perplexed by terms like "RAM" or "web browser," you're not alone. Many seniors who did not grow up in the digital age may be perplexed by these terms. This is where this glossary comes in handy. We've compiled a list of common tech terms with simple explanations for the senior audience.

Antivirus: Software designed to detect, prevent, and remove malicious software such as viruses, worms, and trojans from your computer.

Application: Software that is installed on your computer and performs specific tasks or functions. They are also referred to as programs or software.

Backup: A secure copy of your data that is solely stored in a secure location to protect against data loss.

Bandwidth: The amount of data that can be transferred from and to your computer in a given amount of time.

Browser: An internet access and navigation application, such as Google Chrome, Microsoft Edge, or Firefox.

CPU: "Central processing unit," the unit that acts as the computer's "brain," performing arithmetic and logic calculations.

Crash: Occurs when a piece of software or hardware fails.

Cursor: The arrow on the screen that is connected to your mouse and is used to perform actions by clicking.

Default: The default settings or programs that come with your computer.

Desktop: Your computer's main directory or working area from which you access other directories and applications.

Disk: The storage device that is built into your computer.

Download: Mean download data from the internet, such as programs, photos, files and documents, or other media, into your computer.

Email: Is an abbreviation for "electronic mail," which is a digital message that can be sent via the internet.

Firewalls: are programs or pieces of hardware that are designed to prevent unauthorized access to a computer network or device.

Hardware: Hard drives, chips, keyboards, monitors, and other physical and mechanical components installed in your computer are examples of hardware.

Icons: are images that represent links to different programs or functions on your computer.

Input device: Any piece of hardware that you use to interact with your computer, such as a mouse, keyboard, microphone, and so on.

Install - Getting software or hardware ready for use.

Interface: Is a device, such as a monitor, or a program, such as a desktop, that allows you to communicate with your computer.

LAN (Local Area Network): is a network of interconnected computers in a specific geographic area, such as a home or office.

Memory: Information saved on your computer.

Menu: A list of options that can perform various functions. Pop-up menus, drop-down menus, and other options are possible.

Monitor: A screen or visual display that is linked to your computer.

Mouse: A piece of hardware that you move your hand around to control the on-screen cursor and click buttons.

MP3/MP4: Is a file format for storing video and audio data.

Network: Is a collection of interconnected computers.

Operating system: Software that manages all other software and hardware on your computer, laptop, or tablet, ensuring that all files, programs, and processes have efficient and adequate access to the hard drives, processing units, memory, and storage (Windows or MacOS are Operation System)

Plug and play: Hardware that can be plugged in and immediately recognized by the computer, allowing it to be used, such as a mouse, keyboard, hard drive, and so on.

Program: is synonymous with application.

RAM: 'Random access memory' is computer storage that is used to run background processes for various programs, allowing them to run faster.

Router: Is a device that connects multiple computer networks and routes data to its intended destination.

Software: Consists of computer programs and other data.

Virus: A piece of code that can replicate itself and cause damage to your computer or jeopardize its Zecurity. Malware is comparable.

Webcam: is a digital camera that is connected to your computer and can transmit live video to the internet.

Wi-Fi: is a wireless networking technology that enables computers and other devices to connect to the internet and wirelessly communicate with one another.

Window: is a section of your screen that displays the graphics of a program.

Word processor: Is a program that allows you to create, edit, and save documents.

Introduction:

Understanding Windows 11

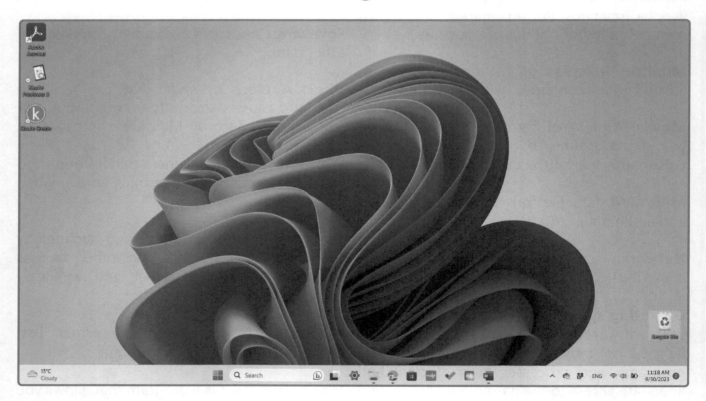

What exactly is Windows 11?

Windows 11 is the most recent version of Microsoft's operating system. An operating system governs all software and hardware on your computer, laptop, or tablet, ensuring that all files, programs, and processes have efficient and enough access to the hard drives, processor units, memory, and storage.

Over the years, various versions of Windows have been launched. Windows 1 was introduced in 1985, and since then, it has evolved into more modern versions such as Windows 95, Windows XP, Windows 7, Windows 8, Windows 10, and the most recent version, which we will discuss in this book. Each version has seen upgrades and modifications to how the operating system looks and feels, as well as more technological changes that operate in the background to improve your computer experience.

Other operating systems for PCs include Linux, Ubuntu, Android, ChromeOS, and macOS.

Each of these operating systems is tailored to the individual requirements of various users. Some are better at office chores like producing documents and emails, while others are better at writing code and developing software.

Operating systems are also intended for different types of devices; for example, smartphones utilize Android or IOS, which are created for mobile devices and are best suited for running little apps, whereas desktops require more extensive operating systems that include a variety of hardware and software.

Windows 11, like other operating systems, provides a graphical user interface. This is a method of communicating with your computer system, mouse, or touchscreen by clicking on various symbols or icons. Character user interfaces were utilized before graphical user interfaces became the norm. To carry out various operations and functions through a character user interface or command-line interface, you would need to type certain lines of code or commands.

Why Should You Use Windows?

Except for Apple products, Windows is one of the most widely used operating systems on the market, and it comes standard with the majority of PCs and laptops. Its advantages over competitors include its ease of use, a large selection of compatible applications, backward compatibility, hardware support, plug and play, and gaming features.

Microsoft Windows is simple to use because it has a standardized design with features that help instruct and guide the user through the numerous functionalities available. Most programs and software, from business and accounting software to music and media apps and even games, are compatible with the operating system.

Software makers must ensure that their apps function with Windows or risk losing a substantial portion of the sales market. **Backward compatibility in Windows simply implies that if you are using earlier versions of a program,** it will almost always run on the most recent versions of Windows, even if it was previously installed on a much older version. It protects the user from losing vital data or games when upgrading the operating system.

Because Microsoft Windows is the market leader, software and hardware vendors must ensure that their products are compatible with the operating system. The majority of hardware components, including hard drives, motherboards, graphics cards, CPU units, fans, mice, keyboards, cameras, and power supplies, will work with the Windows operating system without any configuration. This is referred to as plug-and-play. Finally, the majority of computer games are designed to work with Windows operating systems. Windows provides hardware support for all of the numerous needs that a game may have and can assist in optimizing the game's performance so that you do not have to suffer with bugs or slowness.

Of course, Microsoft Windows has some drawbacks in comparison to other operating systems on the market. Because of all of the capabilities available in the operating system, it necessitates a large amount of resources and appropriate hardware.

If the central processing unit (CPU), hard disk, and memory storage cannot manage all of the processes required to run Windows, the costs will mount. Because Windows is a closed source operating system, the code is proprietary and cannot be edited or changed by the user. In contrast, open-source operating systems such as Linux or Ubuntu allow users to readily modify the code to tailor certain functions or processes to their specific requirements.

This can be a barrier for persons working in highly technical sectors such as software development or internet security. Still, it is not a critical factor for the average computer user. Windows also has rigorous licensing agreements that require users to keep their machines up to date or some features would not work properly, and might involve costly subscription plans.

What is Different in Windows 11 From Previous Versions?

The Evolution of Windows Operating System Throughout History

This analysis aims to provide a concise overview of the evolutionary trajectory and transformative developments of the Windows operating system. By understanding these advancements, users can have a comprehensive understanding of the enhanced functionalities available in the latest iteration.

The initial release of Microsoft's operating system, **Windows 1, marked the inception of the company's foray into the software market.** This inaugural version introduced a rudimentary graphical user interface (GUI) that facilitated user interaction through the employment of a mouse-controlled cursor on the display.

Windows 2 was released a few years subsequent to its predecessor, and it brought forward the novel capability of supporting 16-color visual displays. The aforementioned displays generated distinct information windows that were capable of being shrunk and maximized. Windows 2 also incorporated the use of keyboard shortcuts, as well as the initial iterations of the office software applications Microsoft Word and Microsoft Excel.

The initial release of Windows 3 marked a significant milestone as it became the first version of the operating system to be distributed on a CD-ROM. The year witnessed the introduction of multiple managerial tools that facilitated users in executing diverse activities, hence reducing their need on command-line prompts or lines of code.

Several managers that were originally introduced in earlier versions of the system are still utilized in contemporary iterations. These managers encompass the File Manager, Control Panel, Print Manager, and Program Manager. **Windows 3 provided a palette of 256 colors**, so enabling the modernization and customization of the interface. Additionally, this version of Windows incorporated notable networking capabilities, facilitating the establishment of links among several disparate machines.

Windows 95 is an early iteration that exhibits similarities to contemporary iterations of the operating system, featuring a Taskbar that extends along the lower edge of the screen and a Start Menu positioned in the left-hand corner.

Windows 95 provided users with the capability to establish dial-up connections for accessing the internet, as well as introduced the inaugural iteration of the Internet Explorer web browser. Additionally, it offered multimedia capabilities like the automated setup of various multimedia

hardware components, software programs designed for video, audio, graphics, and image manipulation, as well as enhanced video support featuring greater frame rates and faster processing speeds.

The demand for resources rose when the versions were updated. Windows 98, which was introduced in 1998, required more memory and storage space than prior versions, and many PCs did not come standard with this hardware, necessitating the user's purchase of the necessary upgrades. However, this was a tiny price to pay for the added features and functionality.

Windows 98 supported not only CD-ROMs, but also DVDs and USB flash drives. Additional facilities for managing background activities, including as an update manager, internet sharing manager, and disk cleanup, have been added.

Windows 2000 was released with the intention that it would be adopted for a variety of business uses, as it provided unique business solutions such as file encryption to keep data safe and secure, as well as server capabilities.

Windows XP was by far Microsoft's most successful product, selling nearly 17 million licensed copies in the two months after its debut (Microsoft, 2002). In contrast to Windows 2000, which was promoted to business users, Windows XP was built and designed for the average home user. It had a new look with translucent windows, drop shadows, and adjustable visual styles.

The Start menu was modified and upgraded to provide a two-column layout displaying all installed applications as well as frequently used programs and documents. This version also included a firewall to help protect the machine from internet traffic and the ability to create CDs.

Windows Vista was one of Microsoft's least successful versions, trying to compete with Windows XP's massive success. It enhanced certain areas of visual display and memory management, but it required significantly more hardware, making it inefficient and prone to faults. Many apps compatible with Windows XP would no longer be supported by Windows Vista, and there were other general changes to the interface's design that users disliked.

Windows 7 was released in 2009 and was designed specifically to fulfill the needs of wireless devices such as laptop computers. It included touch, speech, and handwriting recognition, making it easier to use for persons with disabilities, and it supported a wider range of file formats. The taskbar was improved and decluttered once more, helping it function more efficiently and providing the user with a more simplified experience. The file manager was upgraded and optimized, and the system requirements were not significantly higher than in

prior versions. Many customers skipped Windows Vista entirely and went straight from Windows XP to Windows 7.

Windows 8 was a significant risk since Microsoft attempted to capitalize on the touch screens provided by numerous mobile devices, including laptops, tablets, and smartphones. This version did not fare well and was short-lived, but it featured modifications such as a fully revamped layout with a tile-style start menu and the removal of the start button entirely. Although this version offered faster startup times, many users who had grown accustomed to the prior layout and interfaces found it difficult to adjust to such substantial changes.

Windows 10 (yep, there was no version 9) saw a return to the more traditional desktop with the removal of the tile interface. It enables universal apps that function across several devices, such as Photos, Videos, Music, Mail, Calendar, and Messaging. Touch-based and mouse-based interfaces, a new internet browser named Microsoft Edge, a redesigned Start menu, and Cortana integration are among the other improvements. Cortana is a voice-controlled digital assistant that may assist in issue solving and task completion without the use of a mouse or keyboard.

Windows 11 Highlights

Windows 11 includes various new and important features that were not available in earlier versions. A redesign of the appearance and feel, or the interface, is frequently described as more Mac-like. One of the most visible changes is the Task Bar, which remains at the bottom of the screen but, unlike most previous versions, the Start Menu and other application icons are now centered rather than aligned on the left-hand side. The taskbar can be configured to show only the icons you choose, such as a list of recently accessed files, a search bar, or your favorite applications and programs.

A more pastel color palette has been used, and the windows' corners have been smoothed and softened. Windows now has new snap capabilities that let you maximize or shrink windows and arrange them side by side, in a clean grid, or in groups to effortlessly switch between tasks. You can also set up additional virtual desktops, which can significantly boost your productivity. You can create a dedicated desktop for work and business tasks, while entertainment and media can be merged into a second desktop. This reduces the number of distractions while you're working and eliminates unwelcome reminders of work while you're enjoying your amusement.

Windows 11 integrates with a variety of Android apps, which may be accessible via the Microsoft Store or the Amazon Appstore. This means you can use many of your favorite

smartphone apps on your PC, including WhatsApp, allowing for a more seamless transition between platforms.

Widgets are another new feature in Windows 11 that you may use. Despite the fact that they were introduced in previous versions, the developers worked hard to incorporate widgets into the desktop without interfering with other operations or lowering performance.

A widget is a small software that can display dynamic information on your desktop without requiring you to open and launch the app. They can be moved, rearranged, scaled, and adjusted to meet your needs. Calendar, which allows you to check future events, make appointments, or plan your daily duties at a glance; Entertainment, which displays current information on all your favorite shows, movies, and music; Sports, keeping you up to date with the latest scores and athletic highlights; suggestions, which provides important techniques and suggestions to help you enhance your computer experience; and Traffic, which assists you in planning your routes to and from work or the store with built-in intuitive tools that can forecast what time you are scheduled to leave home. There are numerous widgets to choose from, customize, and play with.

Built-in interaction with Microsoft Teams is another useful tool that promotes connectivity between you and your loved ones. Because the application is not pinned to the taskbar, it is easier to use and access. You may easily start a video call with friends and family.

Windows 11 has borrowed some of the convenience of use found in smartphones and tablets by allowing you to change critical settings simply by tapping or clicking on the taskbar's sides. Instead of opening the Control Panel, you may easily alter the brightness, volume, night mode, and access connectivity controls this way. The voice typing function has also been updated, making it more accessible to persons who are blind or have other sorts of vision impairments.

Windows 11 now allows you to play Xbox One games straight on your PC for people who want to play games on their computer. This can be accomplished by either purchasing, downloading, and installing games on your PC or by streaming directly from your Xbox console to your PC. These modifications include changes to how gaming data is stored, which now uses graphics cards instead, making it significantly faster and more efficient to load and play different games.

There are various security upgrades in Windows 11 that you can use. Windows 11 has tamper-resistant silicon chips that are meant to store and safeguard encrypted data. This is useful for folks who use their laptops to store sensitive business information. Through the Windows Hello technology, Windows 11 provides a few various ways to sign into your devices. You can now utilize facial recognition with your laptop or tablet's camera, fingerprint recognition

if your device has one, or your secure PIN number to sign in. Windows Hello makes it easier to authenticate and validate many of your Microsoft-connected accounts.

What Features Have Been Removed in Windows 11?

Many functionality featured in prior versions of Windows have been deleted, which is unsurprising. This is due to the functions being replaced or merged into newer and more modern programs, or because market research has revealed that they are not popular or in demand by the majority of users.

One feature that you may miss in Windows 11 is a movable taskbar. Previously, the taskbar could be dragged and changed to appear on the sides or top of the screen rather than the bottom. The taskbar is now fixed in place with Windows 11. The taskbar menu has also been eliminated, so right-clicking on the taskbar will now only bring up the taskbar settings rather than all of Windows 10's options.

In Windows 10, the taskbar menu that appears when right-clicking has been deleted and replaced with merely taskbar settings.

Microsoft has also disabled the ability to drag and drop files onto taskbar program icons, which previously opened them in those apps.

Though the Calendar stays largely same, Windows 10 included the option to see a list of scheduled events beneath the calendar fly-out that displayed when you clicked on the date/time in the systems tray on the right side of the taskbar. In Windows 11, only the calendar is visible, not events, and this feature has been replaced with calendar and appointment widgets.

The appearance of the Start menu has also changed significantly, with a "Pinned apps" part featuring app icons and a "Recommended apps" section displaying some of the most recently or frequently used apps and files.

The user profiles and a power button are located beneath these sections. Account and user settings, the File Explorer, the Pictures app, power settings, as well as a list of apps with the most recently used icons at the top of the list and a section with live tiles giving app suggestions were all included in the previous version.

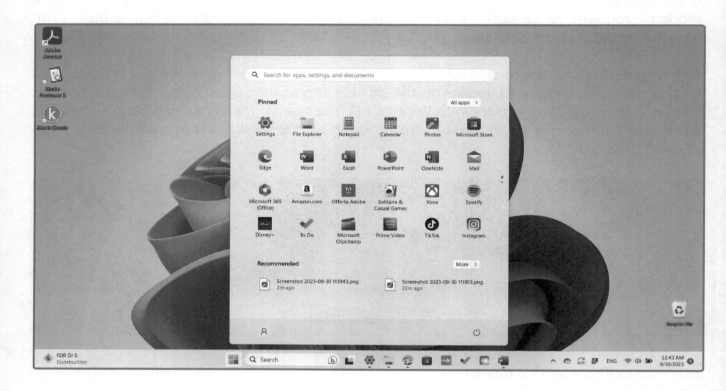

Is Windows 11 compatible with my computer?

The latest version of Windows, like many of its predecessors, will require more resources and better hardware to function correctly. Most desktops and laptops that are currently running Windows 10 may be eligible for Windows 11 when it is released between early and mid-2022. Many older models, however, may be ineligible for this download. Here are some of the hardware requirements for running Windows 11 properly:

- **An internet connection** - If you want to upgrade to Windows 11, you will need to download the operating system from the internet. Many gadgets, however, will be marketed and distributed with Windows 11 already preinstalled.

- **TPM Transfer Module** - this is connected to some of the previously mentioned security updates and is required for Windows 11's security features. Most new smartphones will include this tamper-proof silicon chip, which aids in encryption services.

- **A 64-bit CPU with a clock speed of 1GHz or higher.** This information can be found in the "Device Specifications" option in the Settings app, and it will also be clearly presented when purchasing a new device. The precise significance of this information is unimportant.

- **RAM must be at least 4GB**. Similar to the processor, the amount of RAM installed in your computer can be found in the "Device Specifications" category within the Settings app.

- **A minimum of 64GB of on-device storage is required**. This is the amount of space necessary on your PC to download and install all of the operating system's files, as well as any potential space required for future updates.

The UEFI firmware connects the operating system to the hardware programming. Windows 11 will be compatible with the following CPUs (central processing units):

Intel 8th Gen (Coffee Lake)	Intel 9th Gen (Coffee Lake Refresh)
Intel 10th Gen (Comet Lake)	Intel 10th Gen (Ice Lake)
Intel 11th Gen (Rocket Lake)	Intel 11th Gen (Tiger Lake)
Intel 12th Gen (Alder Lake)	Intel 13th Gen (Raptor Lake)
Intel 14th Gen (Raptor Lake-S Refresh)	Intel Xeon Skylake-SP
Intel Xeon Cascade Lake-SP	Intel Xeon Cooper Lake-SP
Intel Xeon Ice Lake-SP	Intel Core X-series
Intel Xeon® W-series	AMD Ryzen 2000 Series

AMD Ryzen 3000 Series	*AMD Ryzen 4000 Series*
AMD Ryzen 5000 Series	*AMD Ryzen 6000 Series*
AMD Ryzen 7000 Series	*AMD Ryzen Threadripper 2000*
AMD Ryzen Threadripper 3000	*AMD Ryzen Threadripper Pro 3000*
AMD Ryzen Threadripper Pro 4000	*AMD EPYC 2nd Gen*
AMD EPYC 3rd Gen	*AMD EPYC 4th Gen*

This list lists the majority of processors that can currently run Windows 10 (as well as Windows 11).

How to Upgrade Windows 11

If your device is capable of running Windows 11, Microsoft will notify you that an upgrade is available. **You can check for an upgrade by going to Settings > Windows update.** Select Check for Updates. If you are eligible, you will receive the Windows 11 feature update. Choose Download and install. Then, as Windows does the installation process, you must follow all instructions. This can take a few minutes.

Once you've installed Windows 11, you should check for updates on a frequent basis to keep your machine functioning smoothly. These updates can also be found in the same area, albeit Windows will notify you of their availability.

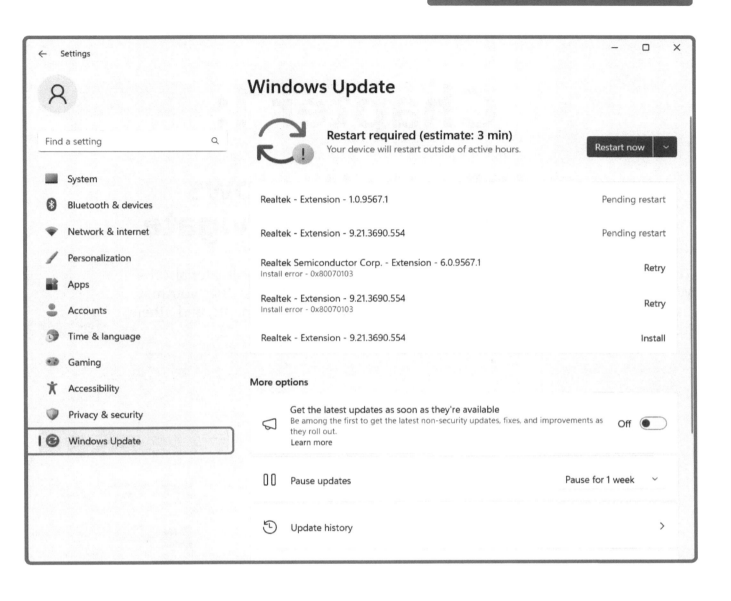

← Settings

Windows Update

Restart required (estimate: 3 min)
Your device will restart outside of active hours.

[Restart now ▾]

R Find a setting 🔍

💻 System

🟦 Bluetooth & devices

📶 Network & internet

✏️ Personalization

📦 Apps

👤 Accounts

🕐 Time & language

🎮 Gaming

🧍 Accessibility

🛡️ Privacy & security

🔄 Windows Update

Realtek - Extension - 1.0.9567.1   Pending restart

Realtek - Extension - 9.21.3690.554   Pending restart

Realtek Semiconductor Corp. - Extension - 6.0.9567.1   Retry
Install error - 0x80070103

Realtek - Extension - 9.21.3690.554   Retry
Install error - 0x80070103

Realtek - Extension - 9.21.3690.554   Install

More options

📢 **Get the latest updates as soon as they're available**   Off ⬤
Be among the first to get the latest non-security updates, fixes, and improvements as
they roll out.
Learn more

⏸️ Pause updates   Pause for 1 week ▾

🕑 Update history   >

Chapter 1:

Using the Windows __File Explorer__ to Navigate

The File Explorer is the primary means of moving through the material on a Windows 11 PC. This is a file management system and browser that you may use to find, manage, and remove all of your files, images, documents, and other items.

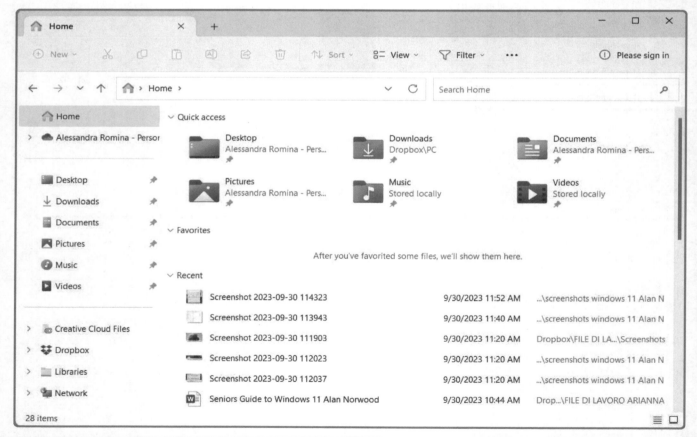

File Explorer

File Explorer debuted in Windows 95 and has been included in every version thereafter, including Windows 11. It is a browser that allows you to navigate through your computer's disks, libraries, folders, and files. It can be used to search for documents, categorize and manage files, and do a variety of other tasks to help curate your computer's library.

File explorer, like the rest of the operating system, has been redesigned, and many of the icons for basic folders such as the Desktop, Documents, Downloads, Music, Pictures, Videos, and disk drives may seem different than you are used to. However, the patterns remain intuitive, and the colors add a splash of color to your File Explorer.

How to Use the File Explorer

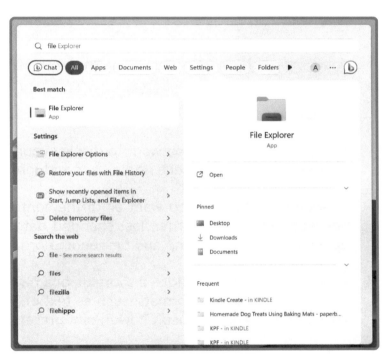

- To **open File Explorer quickly**, use the keyboard shortcut **Win+E** (the Win key looks like the Windows 4-panel logo).

- Select the **File Explorer icon** from the taskbar.

- Start by **typing "File Explorer"** into the **Start menu.**

Using the File Explorer

The File Explorer contains numerous components. The ribbon bar has been removed in Windows 11, and in its place is a command bar with various essential functions such as Cut, Copy, Paste, Rename, Share, Delete, View, and Sort icons.

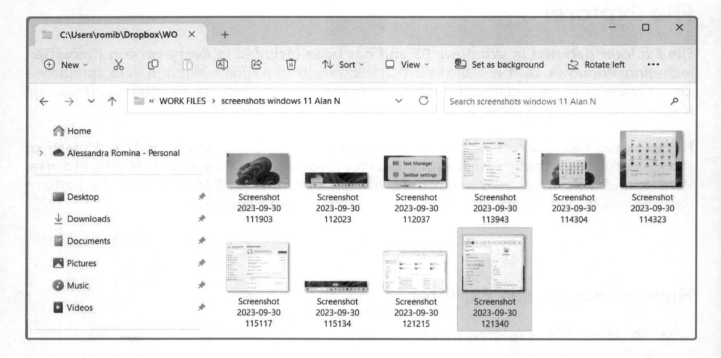

• **View:** Choose how you want to display your folders. You can display huge icons or a list with extra information such as file sizes and formats.

• **Sort:** Choose how you want all of the content in the libraries to be organized. Choose between alphabetical order, last changed date, file type, and more. You may also quickly switch between ascending and descending order.

• **New:** Create a new folder, a shortcut, or a new document by clicking. Several of your most often used document formats, such as text or Microsoft Word documents, Microsoft Excel spreadsheets, and Microsoft PowerPoint presentations, will appear here.

• **See more:** An icon with three little dots appears on the right side of the command bar. The "See more" button is located here. When you click it, a mini menu with further settings and functions will appear. This includes the following:

o **Undo** - to rapidly undo your most recent actions, which is useful if you mistakenly destroy or move an essential document, and the option to pick or deselect multiple files.

o **Pin files to the Quick Access folder** - Any highlighted files or folders are placed in a special library that appears on the left side of your screen when working in File Explorer.

○ Depending on the library you are browsing, some of the options in the command bar will change. When viewing photographs, you will notice image-specific options such as 'rotate' and "set as desktop background." When you look at your drives, you will notice networking tools.

○ Other capabilities include file cleanup, the ability to optimize or format your drives, the ability to add a new network location, map a network drive, detach a network drive, view file or folder properties, or open file or folder options.

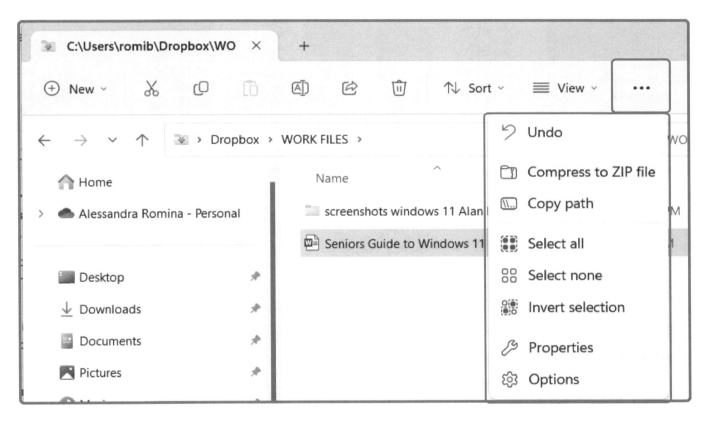

A **context menu appears when you right-click on any file or folder in the File Explorer.** Context menus have also been overhauled, with **new essential options such as Cut, Copy, Rename, Share, and Delete being pinned to the top.** Instead of text, these are represented by simple icons.

The **new 'Share' tool allows you to easily share content with frequently used contacts,** just as on a mobile device. When you press the 'share' button, a menu will appear, outlining how many items you are sharing and offering you the choice to send it to nearby contacts through Bluetooth, email it via the Mail app, or share the content via a variety of other apps.

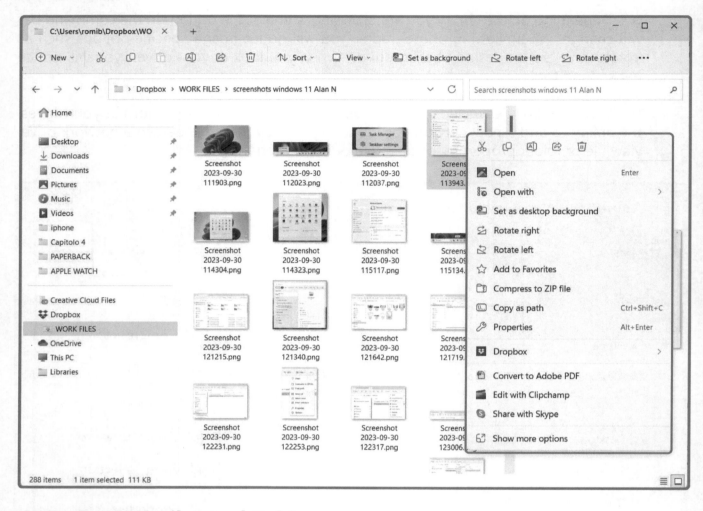

Copy & Paste Files and Folders

Copying and pasting files is easier than ever in Windows 11. With the addition of the copy and paste buttons to the Command bar, you can simply choose and highlight the files you want to copy before pressing the Copy button.

<u>**This copies the content to the 'clipboard.' You can also accomplish this by choosing the information and highlighting it, then pressing Ctrl+C on your keyboard.**</u> Then, in the command bar, navigate to the spot where you want the files or folders pasted and simply click the Paste button. <u>**You may also accomplish this on your keyboard by hitting Ctrl+V**</u>. This will move the desired material to a new location. The original directories or files are not altered by copying and pasting, and you may still view and access them in their original position.

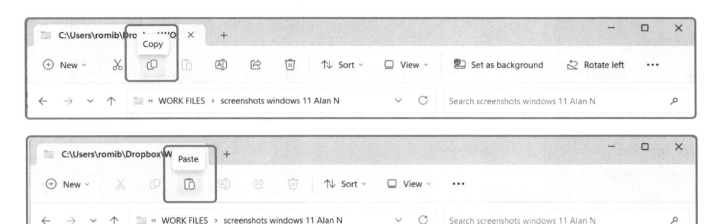

Files and Folders for Cutting

The cutting tool is used to delete files or directories from your libraries, but this content is also saved to the clipboard and can be pasted elsewhere.

It functions similarly to the copying tool. Simply choose the files or folders to be eliminated and press the cut button. **Ctrl+X can also be used on your keyboard to cut files and folders.** Then, navigate to the new site and copy the content. It is critical to remember that cutting the information will remove it from its original spot and will not result in a copy.

Cutting is useful for avoiding the creation of unwanted duplicates, which can clog your libraries.

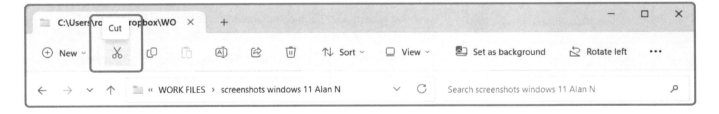

How to Access File Properties

The file properties provide important information such as the file's name, the type of file (such as a Word document, Excel spreadsheet, or JPEG image), the contents of the folder if it contains many subfolders or multiple files, the size indicating how much space it takes up on your disk drive, the parent folder in which the folder or file is located, the amount of free space in the parent folder of your selected folder, and the time and date when the file or folder was created.

You may view the properties of a file or folder by **choosing it in File Explorer** and then using the **"show more" button** on the command line. Remember, this is the three-dot button. This will bring up a little menu with 'Properties' at the bottom. You may also view the file or folder properties by right-clicking on it, scrolling to the bottom of the pop-up menu, and selecting 'properties.'

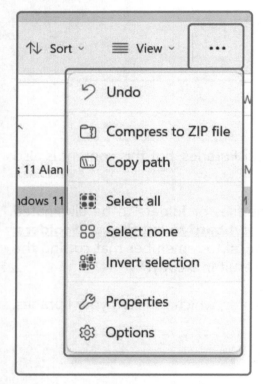

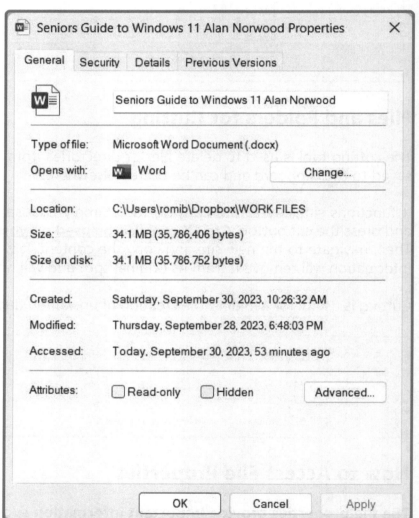

How to Make Use of the View Button

The View button in the Command bar in Windows 11 allows you to quickly move between different types of views. You can view icons in extra large, giant, medium, or tiny sizes, as well as lists, details, tiles, or content.

You can also use "Compact view" to reduce the amount of space between files and folders. This functionality was included since Windows 11 is designed for touch-enabled devices, where greater spacing between files, folders, and icons make them easier to choose with your finger.

This feature, however, can be simply enabled or disabled to suit your needs.

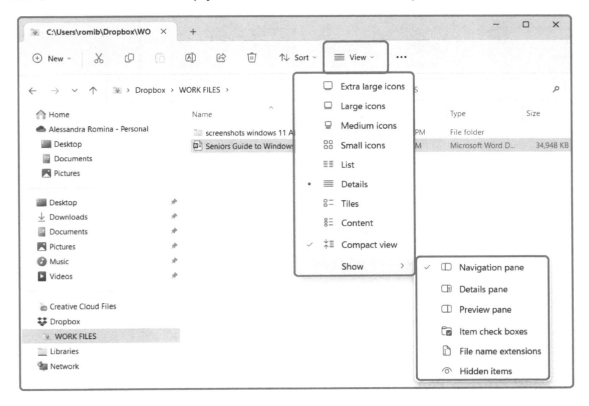

You may also choose what kind of information you want to show in the View menu, such as a navigation pane, a details pane, a preview pane, item check boxes, file name extensions, and hidden items.

The Navigation pane shows on the left side of the window and provides shortcuts to some of your computer's parent libraries, such as the "Quick Access" library, 'OneDrive,' "This PC," and your 'Network.' "Quick Access" contains the Desktop, Downloads, Documents, Pictures, Music, and Videos. You can choose whether to show or conceal the Navigation Pane completely.

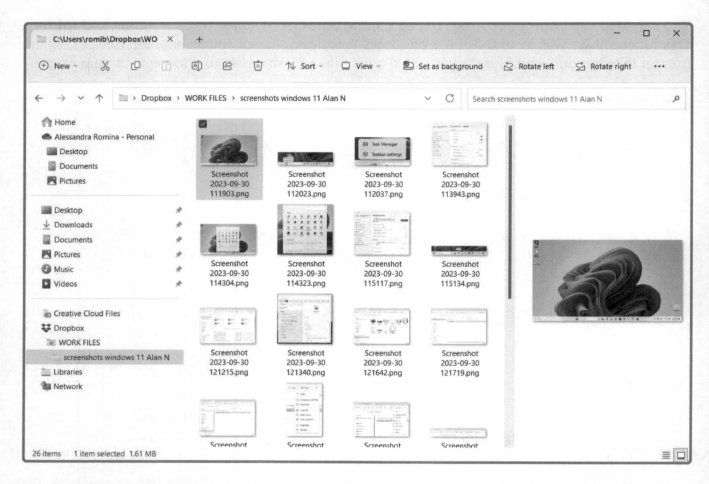

The Details and Preview Panes function similarly to the Navigation Pane, but they appear on the right side of the File Explorer Window. These panes will display information on the file or folder you've chosen. The Details Pane displays information such as the name, file format, last date updated, size, and creation date of your selected folder or file.

The Preview Pane, as the name implies, displays a preview of the currently selected file. Using this function, you can navigate through the preview to see different pages in the manuscript.

The "Item check boxes" feature is new to Windows 11 and was designed with touch-screens in mind. It allows you to choose several files or folders for moving, copying, pasting, or cutting.

When you click this button, small check boxes will appear over all of the items in your File Explorer, which you may check or uncheck. This functionality functions precisely like holding down the Ctrl button while using your mouse to click on various things.

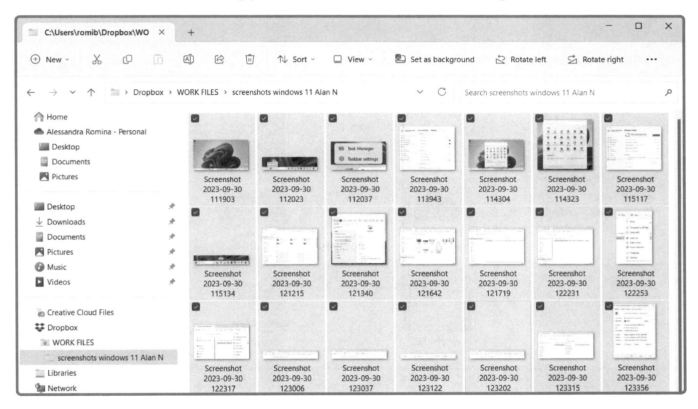

You can now choose to show or hide file extensions in the File Explorer in Windows 11. The file extensions indicate the file format, which informs Windows about the type of file and which application is required to open, interact with, or run the file. File extensions are normally three or four letters long and appear at the end of a file's name. **Among them are JPEG, JPG, PNG, DOC, DOCX, XLS, PPT, and ZIP, among many others.**

Finally, the View Menu allows you to view or conceal "Hidden items." Windows allows you to hide specific files and directories, and many are hidden by default because they are not intended to be updated. They frequently contain crucial system-related data, but any file might be concealed. **Using the "Hidden items" button, you can toggle this feature to show or hide these files.**

How to Make Use of the Sort Button

The Sort button functions similarly to previous versions of Windows, allowing you to arrange the items in your File Explorer in a variety of ways. You can arrange your files and folders according to their name, file type, size, date created, date changed, authors, tags, or title. You may also select whether the sorted material should be displayed in ascending or descending order. Files, for example, can be sorted by size from largest to smallest or smallest to largest. **You can also view information from A-Z or Z-A.**

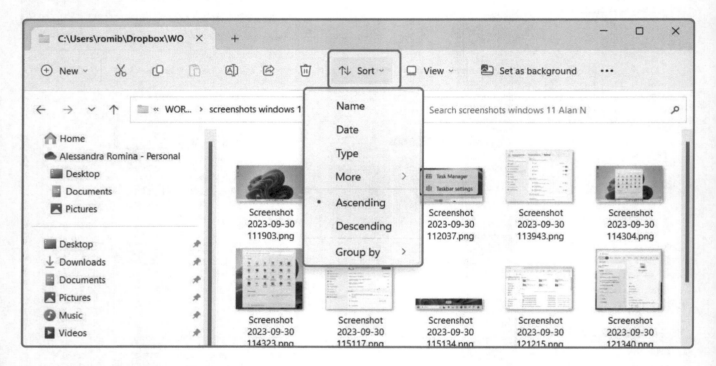

Creating a New Folder

It is now easier than ever to create a new folder in File Explorer. Simply select the 'New' option from the Command Bar's left side. This will bring up a drop-down menu with the option to create a new folder or shortcut. You can also use this menu to generate new files such as Microsoft Word documents, Microsoft Excel spreadsheets, and Microsoft PowerPoint presentations. This operation will launch the appropriate program, allowing you to begin working on the new document.

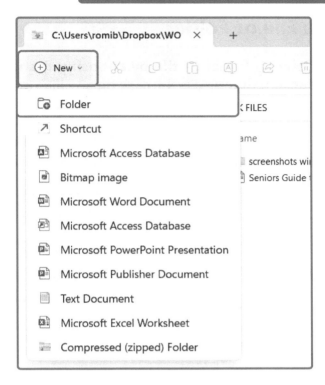

Moving a File From One Folder to Another

There are several ways to move files from one area to another using the Windows 11 File Explorer. The first step is to select the file or files to be moved. You can do this by holding down the Ctrl key while clicking on the files you want, or by utilizing the checkboxes stated previously. Before moving files, ensure that they are correctly highlighted, which may be accomplished in two ways:

- **The first method is just to drag and drop the files into the specified area**. This method works well with a standard computer or laptop equipped with a mouse. Select the files that should be highlighted and drag them to the folder where you want them to go.

- **You can also copy and paste files from one area to another. This can be accomplished by utilizing the keyboard shortcuts Ctrl+C and Ctrl+V**, as well as the control bar's copy and paste buttons. You can also opt to cut and paste instead, which would erase the files from their original location rather than creating duplicates.

How to Get Rid of a File or Folder

In File Explorer, you can delete a folder or file by choosing it and then using the 'Delete' button in the Command Bar. You may also right-click on any files or folders you want to delete to bring up a little menu with the option to 'delete.'

You can also remove a single or more files by pressing the **Maiusc + Canc buttons simultaneously**. Keep in mind that you will not be able to recover the file/files from the recycle bin in this situation.

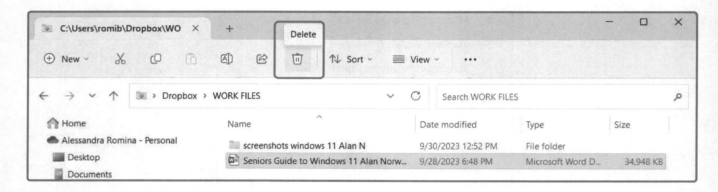

How to Find a File on Your Computer

File Explorer makes it simple to locate a file or folder, regardless of where it is located on your computer. Aside from the Command bar, there is an Address bar on the left and a Search bar on the right. All you have to do is type the name of the file or folder you want into this search field. The results of your search will be presented in the File Explorer window.

How to Reverse or Undo an Action

If you delete a file or transfer something by mistake, you may instantly undo this operation by using your keyboard keys. To undo an action, press Ctrl+Z, and to redo it, click Ctrl+Y.

Recovering a Deleted File or Folder

Like earlier versions, Windows 11 will maintain a temporary copy of all deleted files and folders in the Recycle Bin. To access the Recycle Bin, either click on the icon on your desktop or type **"Recycle Bin"** into the File Explorer's URL bar.

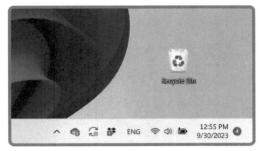

Recycle Bin will open a folder in your File Explorer that contains all of the recently deleted files and folders. Navigate to the file or folder you want to restore, then click it. A button in the Command bar will appear, offering you the choice to restore this file. This action returns the file to its original location, where it can be accessed.

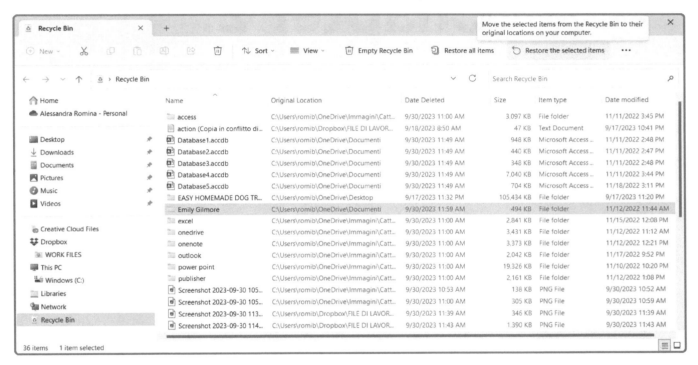

If you cannot find a Recycle Bin icon on your desktop, you may need to adjust a few settings.

- Navigate to **Settings > Personalization > Themes.**

- Scroll down until you reach "**Desktop icon settings.**"

- Make sure the **Recycle Bin checkbox is selected** here.

Chapter 2:

Learn How to Manage Settings

Many settings in Windows 11 may be changed and altered to provide a more personalised and personalized experience whether working or playing on your computer. This chapter will go through how to utilize and modify some of the most significant options.

The Settings App

In Windows 11, the Settings App replaces the Control Panel as the major center for all your customization, installation, connection, account settings, and more. There are several methods to access the Settings App:

1) Navigate to the **Settings icon**, which is denoted by a cogwheel, by clicking on the Start Menu.

2) **You may pin the Settings App to your taskbar by dragging and dropping this icon there.** The Settings App may also be pinned to the taskbar by right-clicking the app icon and selecting "Pin to taskbar." **Click on the Start Menu and type in 'settings'** to bring up the Settings app icon.

3) **Go to the Start Menu and select the "All apps" option.** You may then **look for the Settings App**, which is alphabetically arranged among the other programs.

4) The Settings App may also be accessed by pressing **Windows Key + I.**

5) Finally, o**n the right side of the taskbar, click the Quick Settings button** to open a **small flyout menu with an icon for the entire Settings App** in the lower right corner.

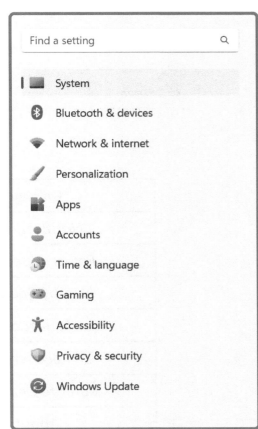

The Settings App displays several settings categories in a navigation pane on the left side of the window and immediately opens up to the System settings.

The following choices will be available in this section: Display, Sound, Notifications, Focus Assistant, Power And Battery, Storage, Nearby Sharing, Multitasking, Activation, Troubleshoot, Recovery, Projecting To This PC, Remote Desktop, Clipboard, and About are some of the features available.

Here is a list of all the choices available in these menus:

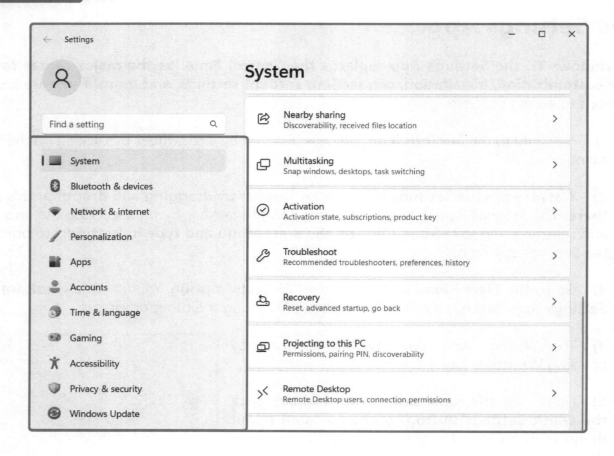

System

Display	Sound
Notifications	*Focus*
Power & battery	*Storage*
Nearby Sharing	*Multitasking*
Activation	*Troubleshoot*
Recovery	*Projecting to this PC*
Remote Desktop	*Clipboard*
About	

Bluetooth & Devices

Bluetooth	Devices
Printers & scanners	Your phone
Cameras	Mouse
Touchpad	Touch
Pen & Windows Ink	AutoPlay
USB	

Network & internet

Wi-Fi	Mobile hotspot
VPN	Proxy
Airplane mode	Advanced network settings
Dial-up	

Personalization

Background	Themes
Colors	Touch keyboard
Lock screen	Taskbar
Start	Device usage
Fonts	

Apps

Apps & features	Offline maps
Default apps	Apps for websites
Optional features	Startup
Video playback	

Accounts

Your Microsoft account	Email & accounts
Your info	Family & other users
Sign-in options	Access work or school
Windows backup	

Time & language

Language & region	Date & time
Speech	Typing

Gaming

Captures	Xbox Game Bar
	Game Mode

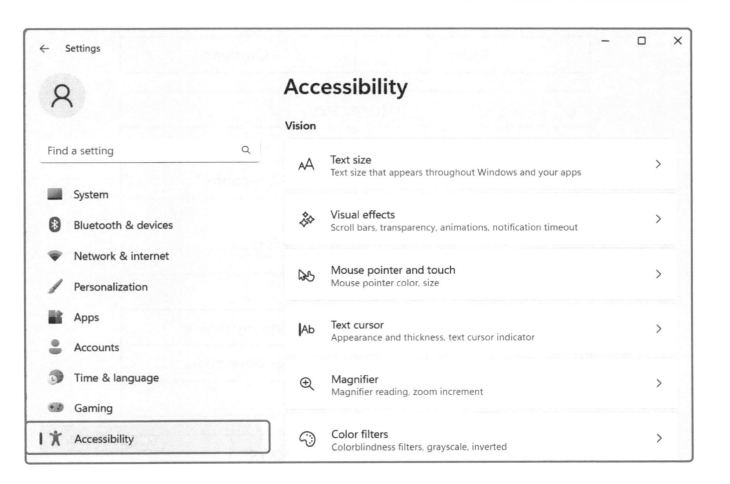

Accessibility

Vision	
Text size	Visual effects
Mouse pointer and touch	Text cursor
Magnifier	Color filters
Contrast themes	Narrator

Hearing	
Audio	Captions

Interaction	
Speech	Keyboard
Mouse	Eye control

Privacy & Security

Security	
Windows Security	Find my device
Device encryption	For developers

Windows permissions	
General	Speech
Inking & typing personalization	Diagnostics & feedback
Activity history	Search permissions

Windows Update

Update history	Pause updates
Windows Insider Program	Advanced options

Accounts

Since the release of Windows 10, Microsoft has encouraged customers to log in to their PCs and laptops using their Microsoft identities. A Microsoft account is a free account that is linked to online services such as OneDrive, Xbox Live, Skype, and Microsoft 365. It is paired with a Microsoft email address. To access all of the capabilities associated with a Microsoft account, you must have an internet connection.

In comparison, you may log in to your computer using a "local account"; this is the conventional method of signing in and is not tied to any email address or internet services. It simply requires a username and password, which will be saved on your computer.

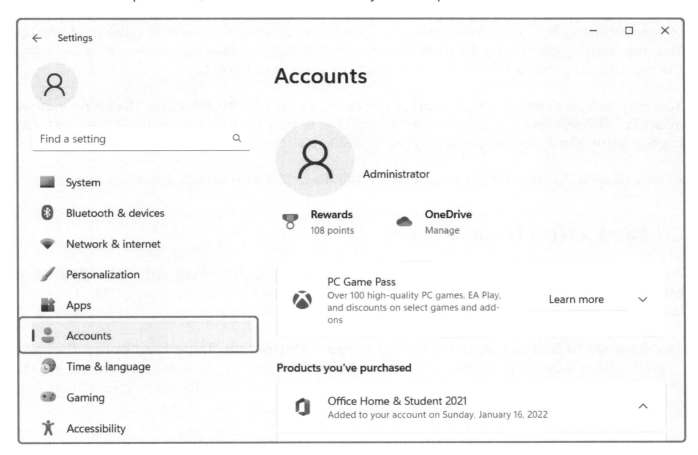

A Microsoft account has various advantages, including access to several of the previously stated online services. It allows full-disk encryption of your system drive automatically, allowing you to safely save and safeguard all of your computer's data on OneDrive. Your subscription and activation data will be saved with your Microsoft account, so you won't have to buy a new copy of Windows if you need to reinstall it, and you can also sync your preferences across different devices.

When you sign in with your Microsoft account, your Mail, Calendar, and other downloadable applications will sync with the linked email address. Finally, with a Microsoft account, you can immediately recover your password through your emails, however retrieving a password for a local account is far more difficult.

How to Register for a Microsoft Account

After installing Windows 11, you'll need a Microsoft account and an internet connection to start utilizing it. If you do not already have a Microsoft account, you may quickly set one up. You may accomplish this by going to the Microsoft website at signup.live.com or by following the instructions provided during the Windows 11 installation process.

You may use an existing email address or create a new one by selecting "Get a new email address." This will take you to a form where you can enter your name, date of birth, gender, and choose a username. You will be prompted to create a strong password. That's all!

All you have to do after a fresh installation of Windows 11 is sign in with this account.

Creating a New Local Account

For security concerns, Windows 11 does not enable you to install without a Microsoft account. However, once the operating system is loaded, you may adjust your settings to use a local account to login into the device instead.

To do so, go to Settings App > Account > Your information. There is an option that says "Sign in with a local account instead." When you click on this link, you will be taken to a page that will prompt you to sign out of your Microsoft account and authenticate your identity before creating a local account.

You can choose a username for your local account, and while a password is not necessary, it is highly recommended. The next step is to click sign-out, which will log you out of your Microsoft account. You can then login back into your device using the newly generated local account settings.

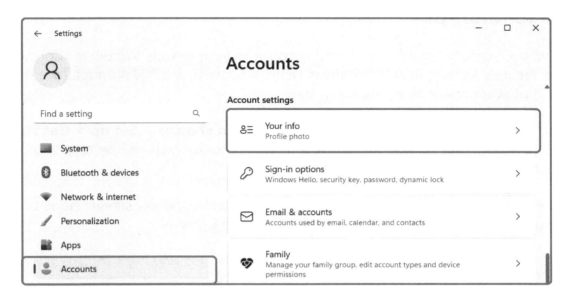

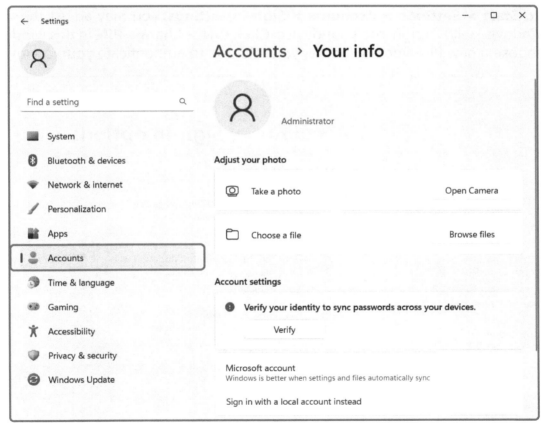

Options for Sign-In

Once you've successfully linked a Microsoft account to your device, Windows 11 provides many options for securely signing in with Windows Hello. A password, a PIN number, face recognition, or a fingerprint scanner are all examples of this.

By going to **Start > Settings App > Accounts > Sign-in choices > Set up > Get started,** you may select how you wish to sign in. To validate your identity, you will be asked to generate a 4-digit PIN code or input an existing PIN code.

Then, if your device has the necessary hardware, just follow the on-screen steps to configure your computer's face recognition or fingerprint scanning services.

How to Change Your Windows Hello PIN

By going to **Start > Settings > Accounts > Sign-in settings**, you may adjust the 4-digit PIN used by Windows Hello to sign into your device. **Click PIN > Change PIN** in this window. Before you may choose a new PIN, you must enter your old one to authenticate your identity.

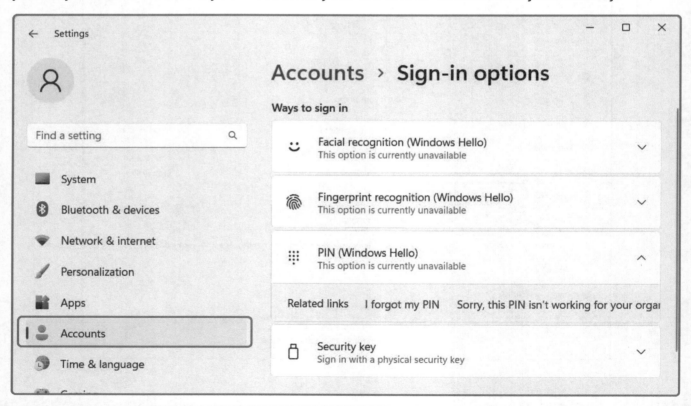

Change the Password on Your Microsoft Account

Microsoft has been pressing its customers to abandon the use of passwords to login into their devices in favor of alternatives like as the PIN system. This is due to the security precautions implemented, as well as the fact that many users use the same password for email and device logins. This implies that if you have activated any of the Windows Hello sign-in options, you will be unable to reset your Microsoft account password in the manner described below.

To change the password for your Microsoft account, go to Settings > Accounts > Sign-in options > Password, and then click "Change your password." Next, enter your current password before entering a new password and a password hint to help you remember it.

If you have enabled Windows Hello sign-in options, the only way to update your Microsoft account password is to go to account.microsoft.com. You then choose "Change password: security." Select your Microsoft account and enter the one-time code that will be emailed to the connected address to confirm your identification. Then, before creating a new password, input your old password. You must also choose a password hint to assist you in remembering it in the future. Then press the Finish button to save your changes.

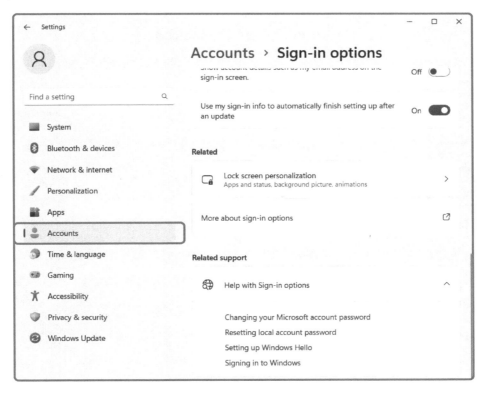

Personalization Settings

By right-clicking on your Desktop and selecting customisation from the pop-up menu, you can simply access any customisation options. Personalization preferences may also be found in your preferences app.

How to Personalize the Taskbar

In Windows 11, the Taskbar is fixed to the bottom of the screen; however, you may adjust many other settings to your desire.

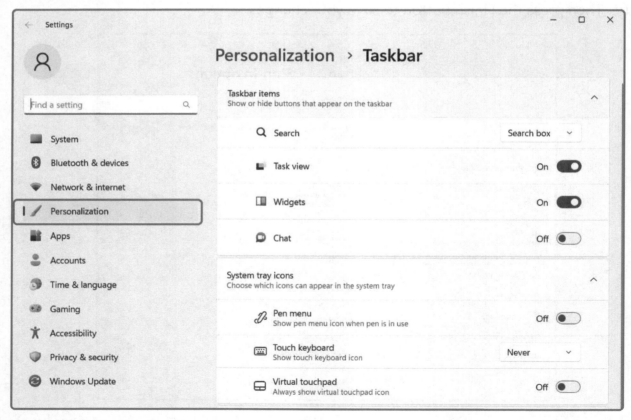

Taskbar Item Alignment to the Left

If you prefer the more typical left-aligned Windows Taskbar layout, you can change these settings in the **Settings App > Personalization > Taskbar > Taskbar behaviors.** The option to position the icons on the left or in the middle of the screen may be found here.

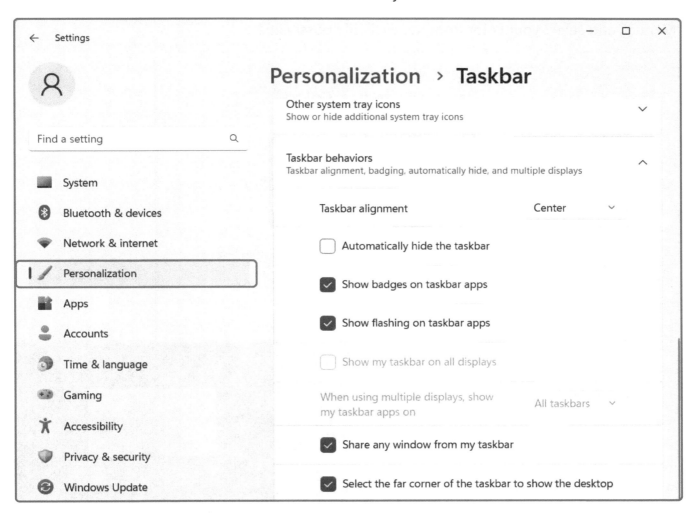

Hide the Taskbar Automatically

You may configure your taskbar to auto-hide so that it vanishes from the screen when you are not using it. When you move your mouse to the bottom of the screen, it will return. This option is also available in the **"Taskbar behaviors" settings.**

Change the Taskbar's Color

You may alter the color or make your taskbar translucent. These options may be found in **Settings > Personalization > Colors.** Choose **'Custom' from the "Choose your mode" drop-down menu and 'Dark' from the "Choose your default Windows mode" menu.** Scroll down and check the "Show accent color on Start and Taskbar" box. Then, change the color accent choice to 'Manual' and select your color from the available possibilities.

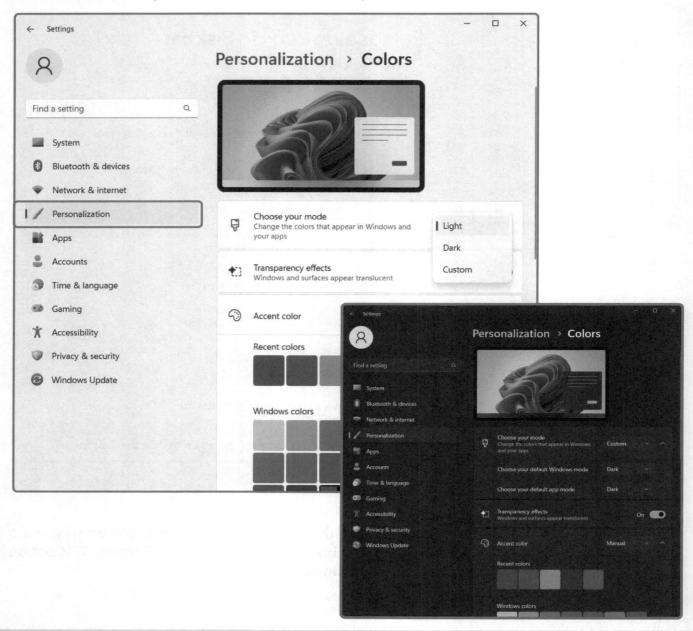

Apps may be pinned to the Taskbar.

Apps may be pinned to the taskbar for quick access. To do so, navigate to **"All apps" in the Start menu. Right-click the icon and choose "Pin to taskbar."** If you don't see this option, look for 'More.' Click this button and then choose "Pin to Taskbar."

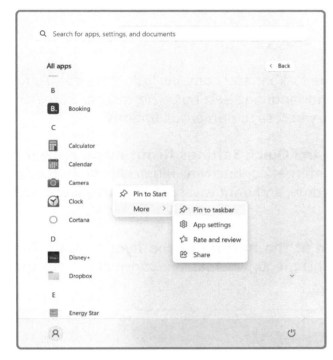

You may also pin desktop programs to the taskbar by right-clicking on the icon and selecting **"Pin to Taskbar."**

Similarly, if you have an app open and running, its symbol will appear in the taskbar, with a line beneath it. **Right-click the icon and choose "Pin to Taskbar."**

Take an App Off the Taskbar

Removing an app from the taskbar is as simple as **right-clicking on it and selecting "Unpin from taskbar."**

Some taskbar icons, including as the **Start Menu, Search, Task View, Widgets, and Chat, cannot be deleted.** The last four applications can be concealed from view. **To hide these apps, go to Settings > Personalization > Taskbar** and look for taskbar items. To conceal these app icons from the taskbar, use the sliders on the right side.

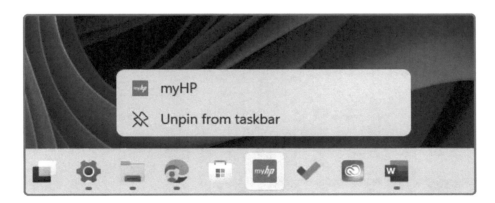

Display Badges on the Taskbar

Certain apps will display badges that you may conceal, such as the Chat app, which will show a counter for all unread messages. This setting may be turned off in the "Taskbar behavior" settings.

Modify the Taskbar Corner

The taskbar corner is located on the right side of the taskbar and contains little icons for useful features such as the keyboard, battery, volume, and language settings. The taskbar corner is intended to minimize clutter while yet providing easy access to numerous options.

When you click on the taskbar overflow corner, the Quick Settings flyout menu appears, displaying the entire array of icons and their state. Internet connectivity, Bluetooth, flight mode, battery saving, focus assistant, accessibility, cast, volume, and brightness settings are all enabled by default.

A pencil icon and a cogwheel icon may be seen at the bottom of the flyout menu. The pencil symbol lets you pin or unpin options from this menu, whereas the cogwheel opens the complete options app.

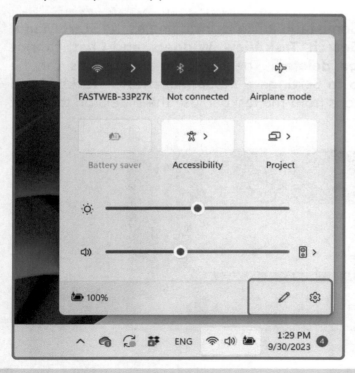
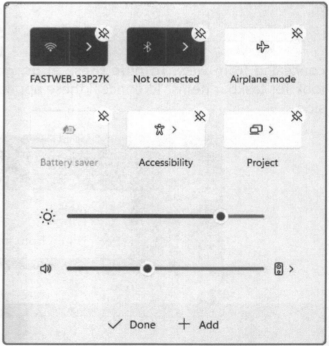

Some system tray icons, such as the Pen menu, Touch menu, and Visual touchpad, can be activated or disabled. This is useful if your device does not have certain input choices.

To activate or disable these icons, go to Settings > Personalization > Taskbar, and then toggle these options on or off.

The overflow tray is located in the Taskbar corner and may be accessed by clicking the little up arrow. In the taskbar settings, under Taskbar corner overflow, you may choose which icon programs appear in this overflow tray.

How to Change the Start Menu

Pinned Apps can be added or removed.

To add an app to your Start menu, choose **"All apps"** in the **Start menu** and look for the app icon. When you find the app you want, **right-click on it and choose "Pin to Start."** Similarly, **to unpin an app from the Start menu, right-click on its icon and choose "Unpin from Start."**

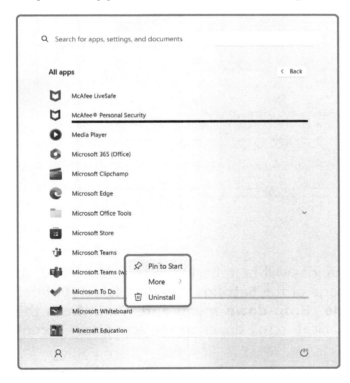
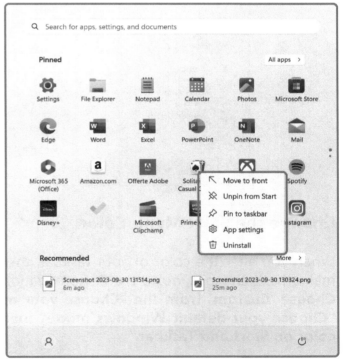

Select which folders display on the Start screen next to the power button.

You may customize the icon that appears next to the power button in the start menu. It's as simple as going to the **settings menu >Personalization>Start>Folders** and clicking on the folders you regularly use.

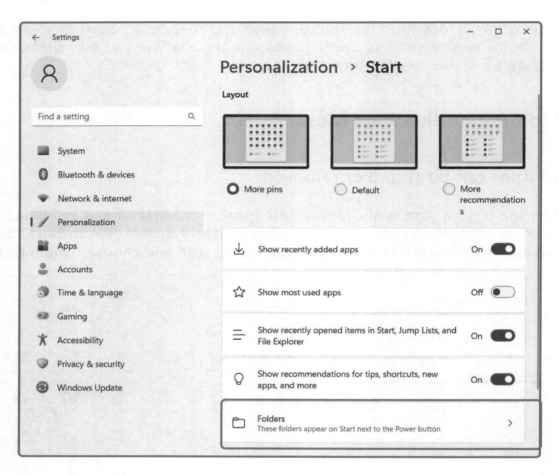

Change the Start Menu Color

When you alter the color of your taskbar, the changes will be reflected in the Start menu. To make these changes, go to the Personalization page of the **Settings app and select 'Colors.' Choose 'Custom' from the "Choose your mode" drop-down menu and 'Dark' from the "Choose your default Windows mode" menu.** Next, scroll down and select **"Show accent color on Start and Taskbar."**

Please keep in mind that if your PC is sluggish while opening and shutting programs or folders, you should disable the transparency effects. This function overloads the GPU and may cause your computer to slow down. Disabling it may help your PC run faster and smoother.

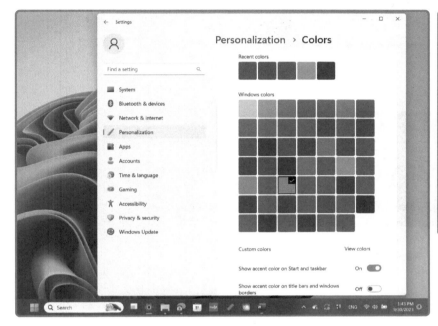 

Hide the Most Popular, Most Used, and Recently Installed Apps.

By default, Windows 11 will display recently installed and most used programs in the Start menu. By selecting **Personalization > Start in the Settings app, you may hide these apps.** You may change these settings here to your desire.

Pin Collections

Unfortunately, with Windows 11, you cannot pin files or folders to the Start menu. You may, however, pin libraries such as File Explorer, Documents, Downloads, Music, Pictures, and Videos. Simply open the Settings App, navigate to **Personalization > Start > Folders, and set the libraries you want pinned to the Start menu to the 'On' position.**

How to Change the Lock Screen

When you lock your Windows 11 device, you will see the Lock Screen, which displays the time and date over a backdrop wallpaper. **To modify the look of your Lock Screen, go to the Settings app and select Personalization > Lock screen.** There are three primary alternatives available here:

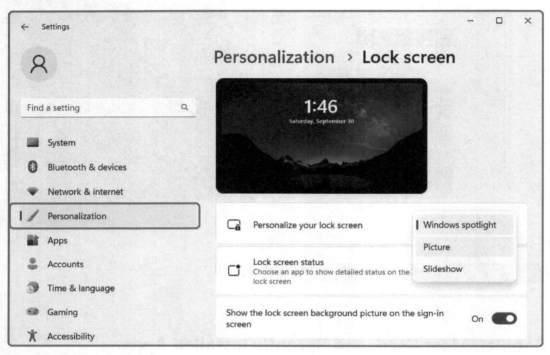

Personalize your lock screen: this option allows you to choose a picture for the lock screen's backdrop wallpaper.

You can use a single image from your Picture Library or a slideshow of several photographs. You may also choose Windows Spotlight, which will automatically import a Bing picture that will be refreshed and modified on a regular basis.

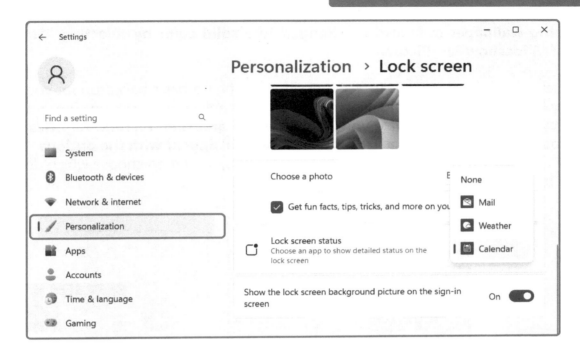

Lock screen status: Using one of the Windows 11 applications, you may choose what information to display on your Lock Screen. You have the option of using 3D Viewer (which works on mobile devices with an accelerometer to produce a 3D Parallax effect), Weather, Amazon, Xbox console companion, Mail, or Calendar. You may only display information from one of these applications on your lock screen.

Show the lock screen background picture on the sign-in screen: This option allows you to disable the display of the lock screen background image when you enter the sign-in screen.

How to Change Your Desktop Background

Windows 11 makes it simple to change the backdrop of your desktop. All you have to do is go to Settings, Personalization, and then Background. This menu contains "Personalize your background," from which you may select Pictures or Slideshow from the drop-down menu. You may use one of the pre-installed wallpaper photos or explore for your own. You may also choose how the image will appear on your desktop based on its dimensions and the size of your display.

If you want to set a slideshow of photographs as your Desktop backdrop, you may simply do so by creating an album in the settings app. There are further choices for how frequently the image changes and if the sequence of the photographs should be altered.

The Desktop wallpaper may also be changed to a solid color by selecting "Solid color" instead of 'Slideshow' or 'Picture.'

You may set various backgrounds for each desktop, such as a basic backdrop for your business desktop but a portrait of your family members for your enjoyment desktop. These options are available by selecting **"Personalize your background" and then Picture. Right-click on the picture you wish to select, and a drop-down menu will appear with the options "Set for all desktops" or "Set for desktop."** Select "Set for desktop," and then choose which desktop you want it to be applied to.

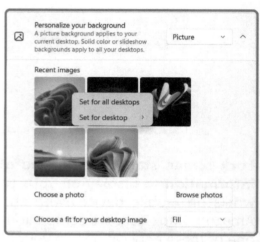

How to Customize the Appearance and Feel of Windows 11

Dark Mode and Light Mode

The taskbar, Start menu, desktop wallpaper, windows, and sound schemes are all changed between dark and bright modes. Dark mode has light writing on darker windows and backgrounds, as well as more muted and quieter noises for various alerts and notifications.

Light mode has black text on light windows and backgrounds, as well as more colourful desktop backdrops and eye-catching alert and notification noises.

You may choose between dark and bright modes by going to the **Settings app's Personalization section and choosing Colors. You'll see the ability to toggle between Dark and Light here.**

Themes

A theme is a collection of settings that affect the background wallpaper, colors, audio, and other customisation choices on your computer. **There are six themes included with Windows 11: Windows Dark, Windows Light, Clow, Captured Motion, Sun Rise, and Flow.** Additional themes are also available for download from the Microsoft website.

Themes may be modified by going to the Themes area of the Personalization settings. You may select desktop backgrounds, color schemes, sound packages, and mouse cursor styles from this menu.

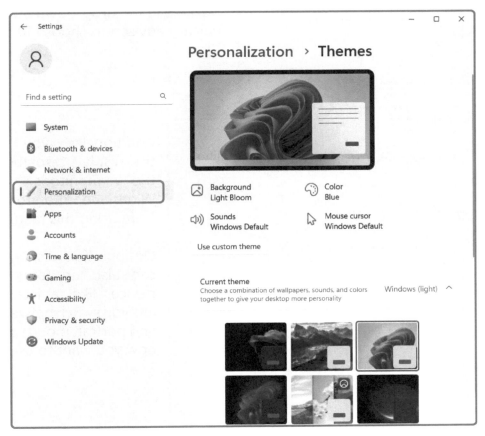

Customed Scaling

The elements on your screen will attempt to be automatically resized by Windows 11 so you can see them clearly and easily. You might, however, occasionally want to make the text, icons, and other elements larger.

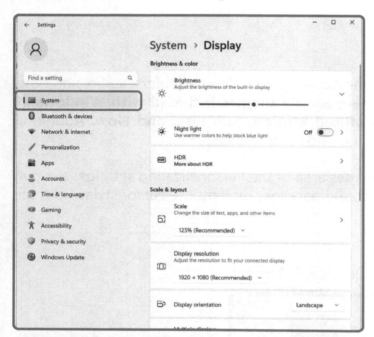

Some computers, for instance, have extremely high resolutions, resulting in relatively small but clearly visible icons and text. Similarly, if you use multiple screens, you might discover that the scaling feature on one device has no use on another.

Go to Settings > Display > Scale and layout contains these scaling options. Options for scale and display resolution are offered here. Numerous scale options are available in the drop-down box, though it is typically advised to choose 100%.

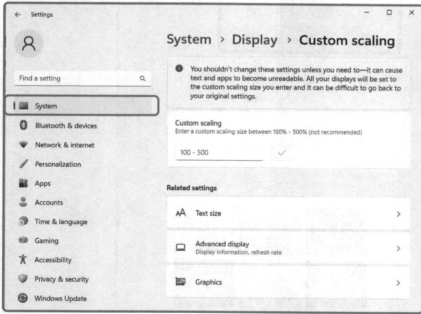

Additionally, you can adjust the display resolution to match the monitor's dimensions. Widescreen monitors can benefit from using this feature.

Options for display orientation can also be found on mobile devices like tablets. This feature lets you switch between landscape and portrait modes depending on how you want to use your tablet.

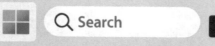

Device Usage

This is a new feature in Windows 11 that will assist and tailor your experience based on how you use your device. Many various things may be toggled on or off in **Settings > Personalization > Device utilization.** Gaming, Family, Creativity, School, Entertainment, and Business are all examples. You may enable one or more of these capabilities, and Windows 11 will then deliver advice, advertising, and other recommendations on services and products to help you get the most out of your experience. If you choose Gaming, for example, Windows 11 will be able to give you Xbox Game Pass trials or recommend applications and games to try out.

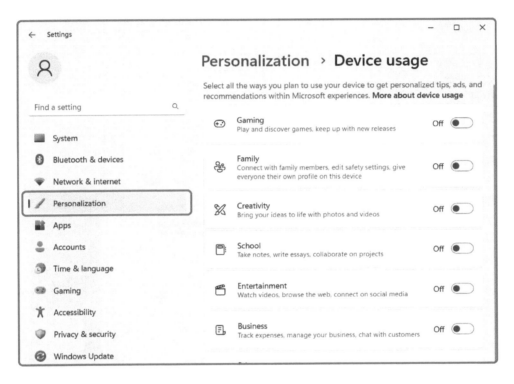

How to Connect Bluetooth Devices

Bluetooth-enabled computers and devices make it simple to connect headphones, speakers, keyboards, mouse, and phones. If your device lacks Bluetooth connectivity, you can purchase USB Bluetooth adapters that plug into a USB port.

First, to pair (connect) a Bluetooth device to your computer, ensure that Bluetooth is switched on. **Go to Settings > Bluetooth & devices and look for a toggle switch.** Then, click the Add device button, and your computer will start looking for any nearby devices. Check that the device you're attempting to link is powered on and in pairing mode. When your device appears on the screen, click on it to link it.

Alternatively, you may open the **Quick settings menu by clicking on the taskbar corner.** There is a **Bluetooth button** here that may be rapidly switched on or off. Your computer will automatically link with any devices in range that have already been paired.

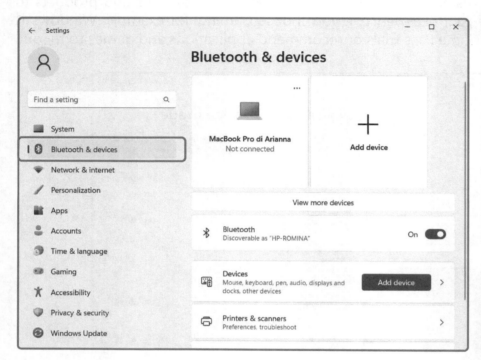

Installing a Scanner or Printer

Network or wireless printers can be quickly discovered by Windows 11 and all necessary drivers can be downloaded. Ensure the new printer or scanner is turned on, connected to the computer or network, or that the wireless connection is properly enabled before installation.

Then select **Printers & Scanners under Settings > Bluetooth & Devices.** To start searching for the device in Windows 11, click the **Refresh button.** Your printer or scanner should be listed under its name. Your printer or scanner will be set up and ready to go when you choose it.

You must try an alternative if your printer or scanner does not appear in the list. With older models, this is possible. **To manually add a printer, click "The printer that I want isn't listed".** Connect the printer or scanner and install the necessary drivers by following the on-screen instructions. Make sure your wireless printer is connected to the same network as your computer if you have one.

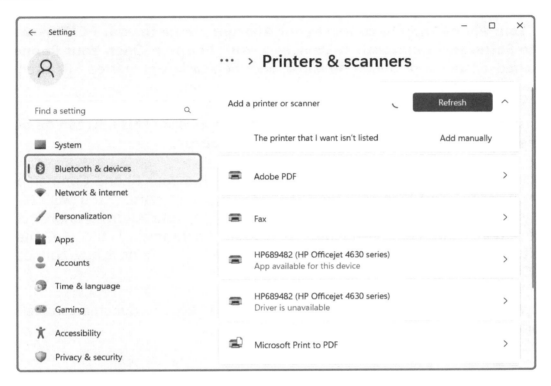

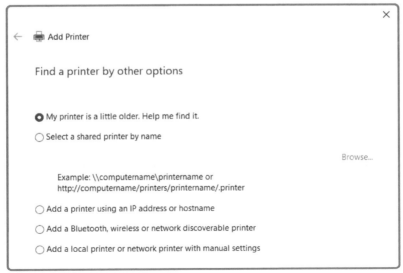

How to Connect an Android Phone to a Computer

With Windows 11, It's easier than ever to remain connected with your Phone by "Your Phone" app. Connect your Android phone to your computer to quickly sync images, videos, texts, calls, alerts, and other data.

Open the "Your Phone" app to connect your Android phone to your PC. This may be done by going to Settings > Bluetooth & Devices > Your Phone > Open Your Phone. Once the app is launched, ensure your phone is nearby, and then click "Get Started." Before proceeding, you may be prompted to check in to your Microsoft account.

You must first install your phone's "Your Phone Companion" app. **This app can be downloaded through the Google Play store or via www.aka.ms/yourpc.**

After installing the app, select the box next to "I have the Your Phone Companion - Link to Windows App ready," and then click the "Pair with QR code" button. You will see a QR code appear on your device. Open "Your Phone Companion" on your Android phone, choose "Link your phone and PC" and then " Continue." Point your camera towards the computer screen so that the software can scan the QR code. Then click 'Done.' Your phone is now connected to your PC. Select 'Continue.'

You can now launch the "Your Phone" app on your PC and access your smartphone's messages, alerts, media, and call features.

How to Use a Wireless Display to Project

Wireless displays are used to effortlessly project the screen of your computer onto a second display, such as a bigger monitor or certain smart TVs.

Visit Settings > Apps > Optional features > Add an optional feature > View features to activate this feature. In the search bar, type **"wireless display."** To pick this option, tick the box and then hit Next. After selecting Install, Windows will download and install the necessary software. You should not notice **"Wireless display" in the Apps settings' Optional features section.** You may need to restart your computer before these adjustments take effect.

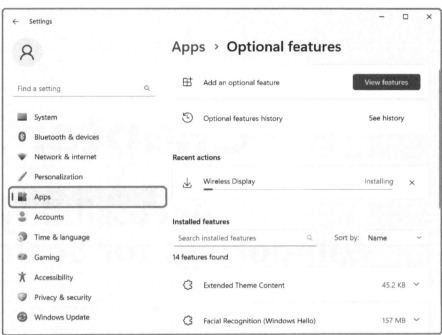

Go to Settings > System > Projecting to this PC to configure your wireless projection. Look for the "Always Off" drop-down menu and adjust it to "Available everywhere on secure networks" or "Available everywhere". Then, select the option labeled "Launch the Connect app to project to this PC." You may now connect any device to your Windows 11 PC that is on the same network.

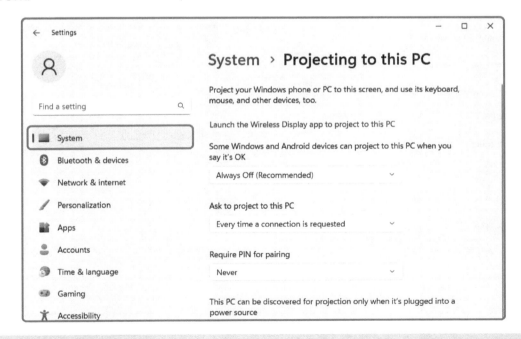

Chapter 3:

Accessibility
(Important for Senior Users)

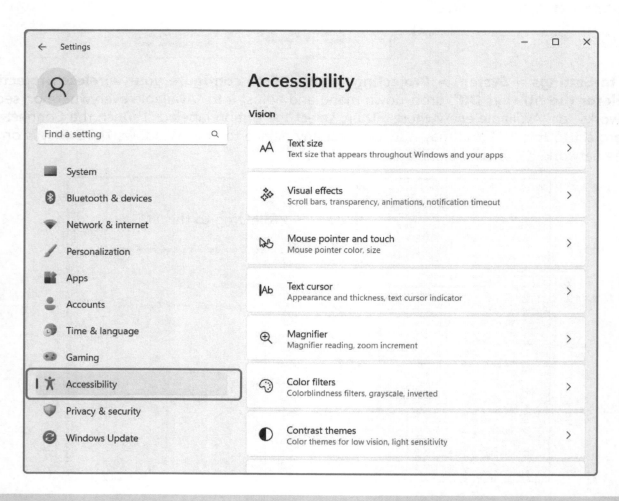

Contrast Themes

Contrast themes were added to Windows 11 to improve accessibility for those with visual difficulties, although anybody may use them. These have a strong contrast between design components to make text, windows, and cursors easier to see. Aquatic, Desert, Dusk, and Night sky are the four default contrast themes.

The contrast themes may be found in Settings > Accessibility > Contrast themes.

<u>**You can switch between high contrast and regular themes using the keyboard shortcut: Left Alt + Left Shift + Print Screen.**</u>

Additional Customization Options

Keyboard with Touch

Windows 11 includes a new and enhanced touch keyboard built for use with touch-enabled devices such as tablets and some laptop computers. It is highly customizable, with handy features like as new finger motions, rounded key edges, a grip tab, an improved layout, an emoji panel with GIFs, and integration with the clipboard to show objects copied.

Personalization > Text input >Touch keyboard contains the options for the touch keyboard. You may change the size of the keyboard here or revert it to its original size. The keyboard themes allow you to select from various design options and incorporate a picture for the keyboard backdrop.

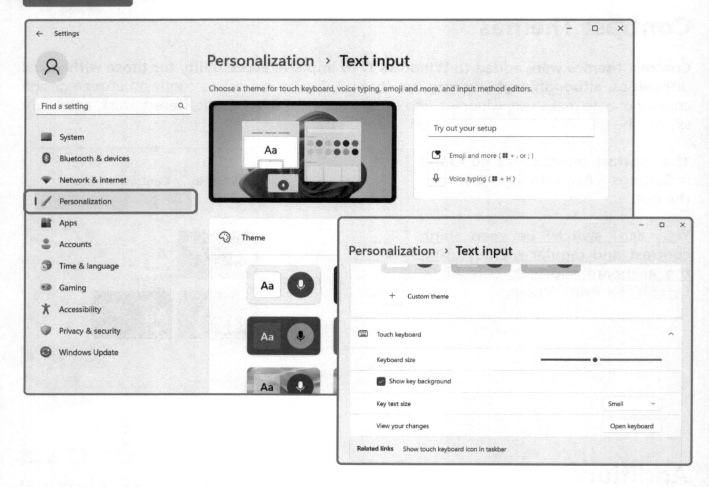

Light, Dark, Color Pop, Tangerine Tides, Lilac River, Indigo Breeze, and Green-Purple are among the sixteen themes available in Windows 11. Each of these themes may be customized, or you can build your own, by going to Keyboard themes **Settings > Custom theme option > Edit.** This feature allows you to modify the text color of the keys, key background color, key transparency level, and keyboard backdrop color. You may also use a picture as the keyboard backdrop.

Fonts

The default font in Windows 11 is Segoe, and it cannot be altered; however, the font size may be readily adjusted. Go to **Settings > Accessibility > Text size** to increase the text size. This will modify the font size in all windows and programs that you open.

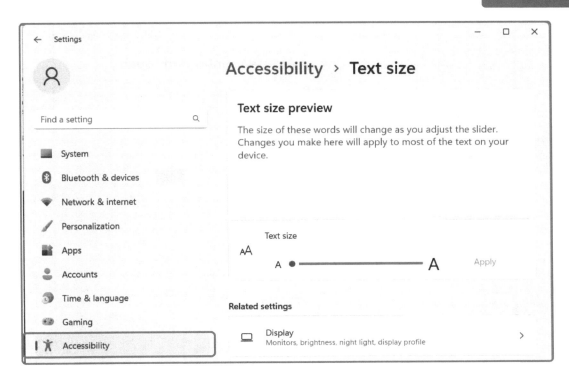

Manage Visual Effects

Visual Effects Windows 11 has animations such as programs shrinking into the background when minimized.

These effects might be annoying or even hazardous, but you can disable them in the options. You may alter the settings for Always show the scrollbar, Transparency effects, Animation effects, and Dismiss alerts after this length of time in the **Accessibility settings under Visual effects.**

Touch and Mouse Pointer

The mouse pointer's appearance on your screen can be modified to make it easier to see.

You may modify the style and size of your mouse pointer under Settings > Accessibility > Mouse pointer and touch.

If you have a touch screen device, you may also change the size and color of the touch indication to make it easier to see.

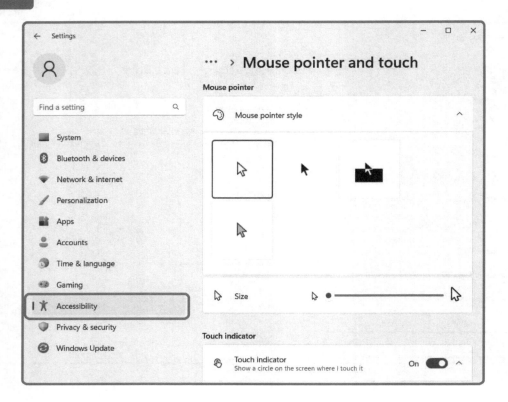

You may also change the cursor's speed, referred to as **"mouse sensitivity."** This helps you move your cursor around the screen more quickly but can also reduce precision.

To adjust the speed of your pointer, go to Settings > Bluetooth & devices > Mouse and drag the slider to the desired speed.

You may also change your primary mouse button from left to right in this menu, and you can alter the scrolling settings on your mouse using the wheel.

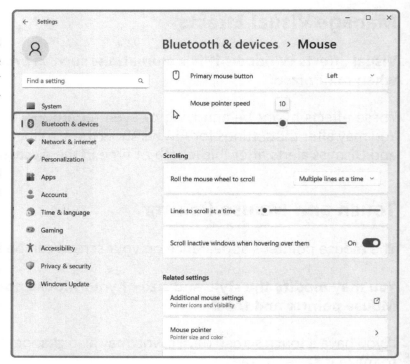

You can scroll down numerous lines at once, or you can configure your mouse such that rotating your mouse wheel only scrolls down one line at a time.

Color Filters

Windows 11 has many color filters to help persons with color blindness or other visual issues view all of the components on their displays. These may be found under **Settings > accessibility > Color filters**.

You'll see a color filter preview with a color wheel, a picture, and some color scales. Windows 11 has grayscale, inverted grayscale, and an inverted color filter, as well as a red-green filter for individuals with poor green vision (deuteranopia), a red-green filter for those with weak red vision (protanopia), and a blue-yellow filter for persons with tritanopia.

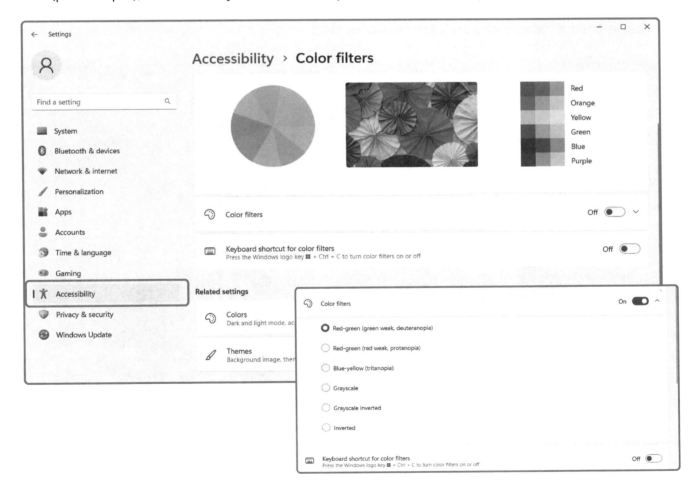

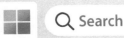 

Chapter 4:

Getting to Know Your Desktop

The Desktop is the central place for all of your computer's activities. Here are visible the taskbar and Start menu. The start menu is accessed by clicking on the windows icon while the taskbar is the bar where all applications are located.

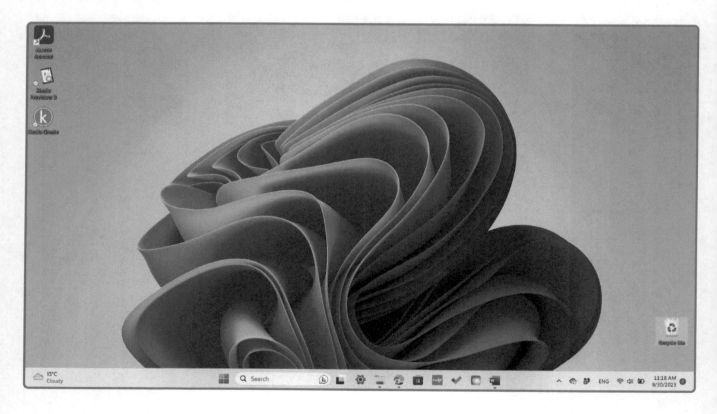

How Does the Desktop Work?

How to Modify the Time and Date

To set or change the time and date, right-click on the clock on the right side of the taskbar corner.

There will be a little pop-up menu; choose **"Adjust date and time;"** this will open the Time and date settings in the Settings app.

Choose **"Set time automatically,"** which will sync your PC with data obtained online. You will need to sync your computer on sometimes to keep it up to date.

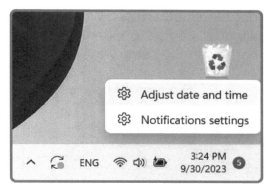

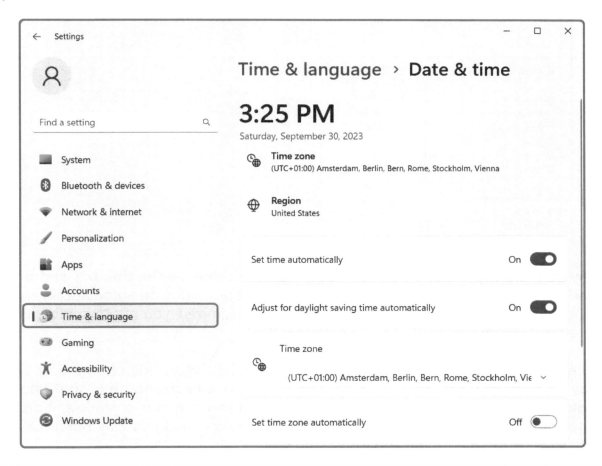

Windows Relocation and Resizing

By clicking and dragging the Title bar at the very top of the window, you may move it about on your desktop. Resizing a window is as simple as moving your mouse to the window's boundaries, either on the top or bottom, where your pointer will transform to a little icon with double-sided arrows. When you see these double-sided arrows, click and then pull or push the window's edge to extend or reduce it to the size you want. You may also drag the window's corners in the same way.

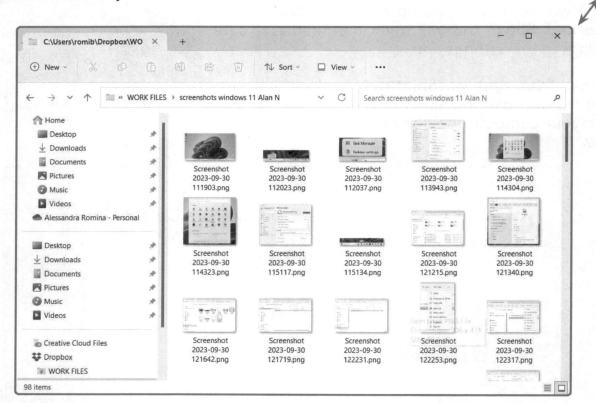

You may also modify the size of your windows by clicking on the title bar and dragging the window to the top of your desktop. This causes the window to automatically maximize, extending to fill the whole screen. When a window is maximized, you may minimize its size by clicking on its title bar and dragging it downward.

There are also three (occasionally four) buttons on the right-hand side of a window's title bar that may be used to resize windows. **The first button is a horizontal line that allows you to shrink or maximize a window by clicking it.** When you minimize a window, it disappears completely from view. The program is still open and running, and you may bring the window back into view by clicking on the app icon in the taskbar.

Finally, Windows 11 now has a new feature called Snap Windows. Hover your mouse over the second button on the right-hand side of a window's title bar to access this function. This will open a little menu with several layout options, such as side-by-side and grids. Move your mouse pointer over these layouts to choose how you want your active window to be organized.

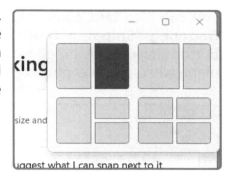

Snap Windows may be enabled or disabled in **Settings > System > Multitasking > Snap Windows.**

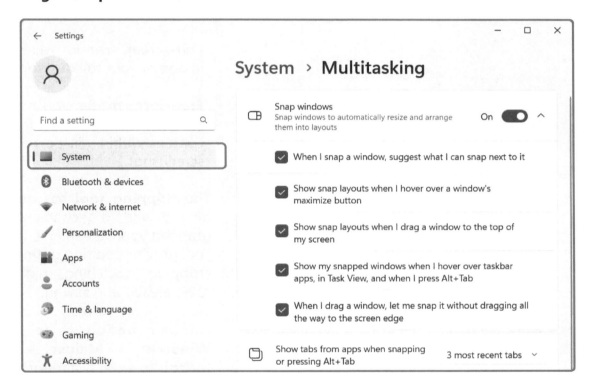

What is a Screenshot?

Taking a screenshot entails photographing your whole desktop and saving it to your computer's clipboard. Simply hit the PrtSc (Print Screen) button on your keyboard to accomplish this. Then, paste your screenshot into any tool that accepts images, such as Microsoft Word, Adobe Photoshop, or Paint 3D. Right-click and select Paste, or use the keyboard shortcut Ctrl+V to paste the picture. **If you simply want to capture a picture of an active window, press Alt+PrtSc and repeat the process.**

You can also take screenshots with the Windows 11 Snipping tool, which you can get by Googling "Snipping Tool" in the Start menu. At the top of the program, there are three buttons: New, Rectangle Mode, and No Delay. When you select Rectangle mode, a drop-down menu with several capture options appears:

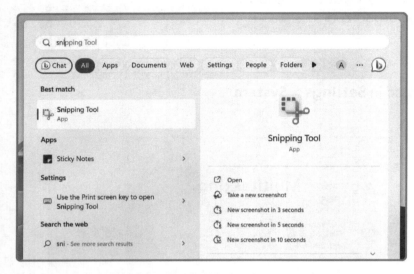

Rectangle mode allows you to create a rectangle with your mouse over the area you wish to capture in a picture.

Window mode will capture a screenshot of the currently active window.

Full-screen mode will capture an image of your full desktop.

Free-form mode, you may use your mouse to design any shape, and the content within will be recorded as a screenshot.

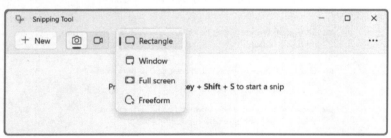

The **snipping tool** has delay options of 3, 5, and 10 seconds. After you've grabbed your screenshot, the Snipping Tool provides editing options including cropping, sketching, highlighting, a ruler, eraser, and saving.

Another option is to utilize the Windows + Maiusc + S combo button to snap a screenshot. You will be able to personalize the screenshot that appears in the notification window.

You may store your print screen in a customized folder here. After taking the screenshot, you may use **ctrl + c and ctrl + v to copy and paste it.**

Creating a Secondary Desktop

Multiple desktops can be created using Windows 11. Create multiple desktops by selecting the **"Desktop icon" from your taskbar.** To see your current desktop and an additional icon with a plus sign, hover your mouse pointer over the taskbar icon to bring up a small pop-up.

Click the plus sign (+) to create a new desktop.

You can switch between these desktops with your open windows. Just right-click the window's title bar and drag it to the Desktop icon on the taskbar. Little windows will start to appear. Release the mouse button, then drag the window to the desired Desktop.

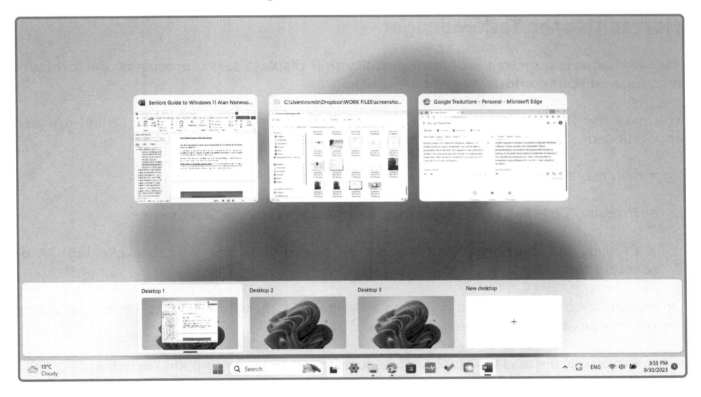

How to Switch Between Open Apps Quickly

If you have many program windows on your desktop, you may effortlessly cycle among them using Alt+Tab.

This will display an overlay screen with each of your windows shown. The active window will be highlighted. Continue holding the Alt button while hitting the Tab button to cycle through the numerous app windows and choose a different one.

When you find the one you're searching for, just let go of the Alt and Tab keys. In this overlay screen, you may also use your mouse to click on different windows.

Pressing Win+Tab also displays open windows. This will launch the Task View, which will display all of your open programs. You may browse to a separate window using your arrow keys and then press Enter to open the selected program, or you can click on it with your mouse.

How to Use the Task Manager

Task Manager is a system monitoring utility that displays tasks, processes, performance metrics, and your computer's general health.

You may use it to examine how much resources an app is consuming, to end a frozen application, or to block an app from starting when you boot up your computer.

- You may **access Task Manager** by: pressing **Ctrl+Alt+Delete**;

- **Pressing Ctrl+Shift+Esc; entering 'Task Manager' in the Start menu**

- Pressing the **Windows+R keys** and then **typing 'taskmgr'** and then **clicking OK or pressing the Enter key.**

On the left side of Task Manager, you'll find a Navigation pane with Processes, Performance, App History, Startup applications, Users, Details, and Services:

- **Processes:** displays the number of resources used by your programs, including CPU, GPU, memory, disk, and network consumption.

- **Performance:** displays real-time graphs of resource utilization information for various programs.

- **App history:** allows you to see how much network and CPU resources certain Store apps have utilized.

- **Startup:** displays a list of programs that will launch and run automatically when you switch on your computer and sign into your account.

- **Users:** displays the number of resources consumed by the various user accounts on your computer.

- **Details:** displays more detailed information about your apps.

- **Services:** displays information about some of the background processes necessary to execute the applications on your computer.

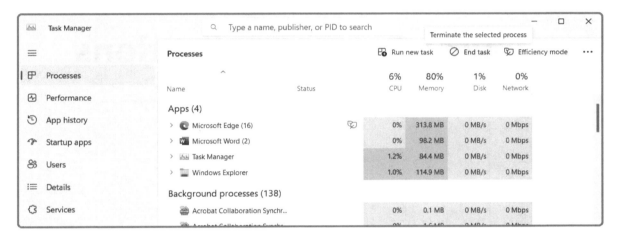

To terminate an unresponsive or frozen program, go to Processes, select the app in the list, click on it, and then **click End Task in the Task Manager's bottom right corner. You may also right-click the program and choose "End task" to compel Windows 11 to terminate it.**

At the bottom left of the Task Manager, you'll notice a "Fewer options" button. By using this option, you may minimize the amount of information displayed, displaying just active programs and omitting any background activities. You may close an app by selecting it from this more streamlined list and then clicking End Task in the bottom right corner of the window.

Click on Startup applications and navigate down the list to prevent an app from starting on startup, which might cause your computer to become much slower. Identify any apps that can be deleted, right-click on them, and choose 'disable' to prevent them from launching when your computer boots up. Make certain that no critical Microsoft systems or hardware applications are disabled. These may be identified since Microsoft Corporation is listed under Publisher.

Chapter 5:

How to Setup Applications

Installing Google Chrome

Despite the fact that Windows 11 includes its own internet browser, Edge, many users choose to utilize Google Chrome for all internet-related activities. You will need to use your edge browser to download Google Chrome.

In the address bar, type google.com/chrome and press enter. You can alternatively type "Google Chrome" into the search field and press enter, then click on the first result to be taken to a download page. Select Accept and Install after clicking the download icon.

Open File Explorer on your desktop, navigate to the Downloads folder, then double-click the installation package to install Google Chrome. The installation process will prompt you to build a desktop shortcut and a taskbar app icon. If you don't want shortcuts, deselect these options.

How to Set Google Chrome as Your Primary Browser

When you set a default browser, that browser will open whenever you click on an online link. To make Google Chrome or another browser your default, navigate to Settings > System > Applications > Default applications.

Type 'Edge' into the search field to see all the links and file kinds for which Edge is the default program. You must click on each of these URLs and file types and change your default browser to Google Chrome. To confirm your selection, click OK.

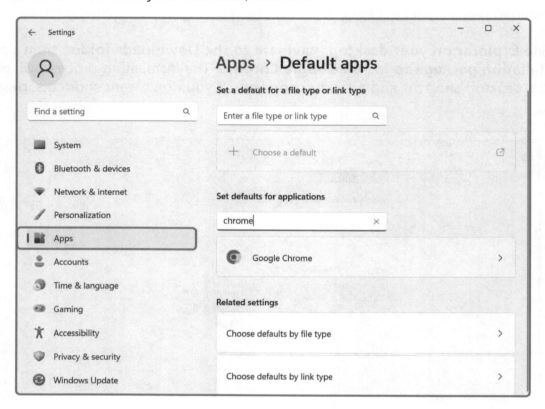

How to Download and Install Any Software Onto Your Windows 11 Computer

Any software you want to install on your PC may be found and downloaded using an internet browser such as Google Chrome. Antivirus software, browsers, VPN (virtual private network) services, office and productivity apps, media players, photo and video editors, PC repair tools, email clients, backup and recovery aides, file management systems, and social programs are examples.

These are some of the best and most dependable solutions for each of these software types:

- **Antiviruses**
  - Avira Antivirus
  - Kaspersky Internet Security
  - Norton 360

- **Browsers**
  - Google Chrome
  - Microsoft Edge
  - Mozilla Firefox

- **VPN services**
  - NordVPN
  - Express VPN

- **Productivity/office**
  - Microsoft Office 365
  - Google Suite
  - Apache Open Office

- **Media players**
  - VLC Media Player
  - GOM Player
  - MediaPlayer Classic

- **Photo and video editors**
  - Adobe Creative Suite
  - Canva (Webapp)
  - Clip Studio Paint

- **PC repair tools**
  - Wise Registry Cleaner

- **Email clients**
  - Microsoft Outlook
  - Gmail (Webapp)

- **File management**
  - Total Commander
  - Directory Opus
  - File Viewer Plus

- **Social**
  - Zoom
  - Teams
  - Skype

You can locate the software you require by typing the name and the word **"download"** into the search bar of your browser.

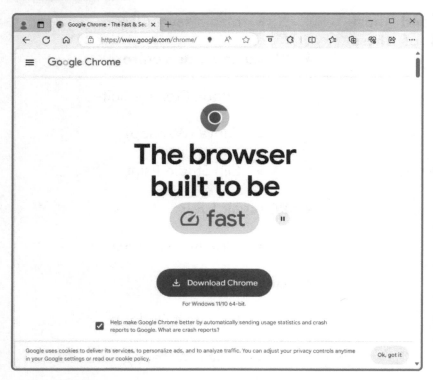

Make sure to click the link that directs you to the software developer's reputable website.

Payment is usually required before downloading and installing many programs, including Microsoft Office 365 and numerous Adobe products.

You will be directed to a download link with instructions on how to correctly install the software after completing the payment process.

Verify your computer's compatibility with the program you want to download by looking at its system requirements.

The website ought to provide access to this information. Then, find the download link and agree to any necessary terms and conditions. You can start installing the file once you've finished downloading it. You only need to check a few boxes and click Next, Accept, or Install for the majority of programs.

VLC Media Player Installation

I want to recommend a free app that is great for media playback. With this app you will be able to play movies, videos and audio.

Proceed to download by using your browser. Go to **videolan.org/vlc/index.html** and download VLC or a simple digit on your browser **"Download VLC"** and go to the videolan website.

Click the "Download VLC" icon. Locate the file in your Downloads folder (or any folder you want) and double-click it to start the installation if it doesn't happen automatically.

A popup will ask you "Do you want to allow this app to make changes to your device?" Select a language and installation location after clicking Yes to continue installing VLC. The VLC software is now accessible from the Start menu.

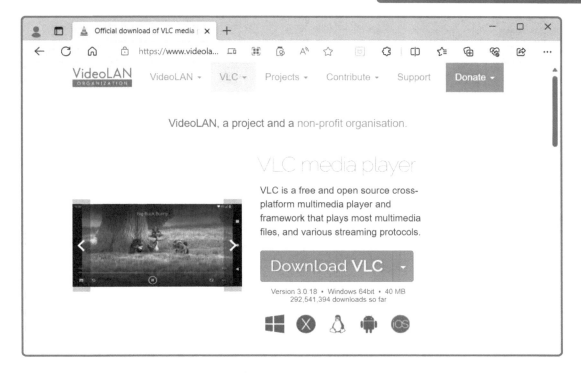

You can make VLC your default media player for different file types by going to Settings > System > Programs> Default programs.

Installing Norton Antivirus

Even though Windows 11 is one of Microsoft's most secure operating systems to date, you can still benefit from utilizing antivirus and internet protection software such as Norton Antivirus.

Kaspersky, like most apps, has a set of system requirements that your machine must meet:

- **2 GB of memory (RAM)**

- **300 MB of free disk space is required to download the application.**

- **1.3 GB of free disk space to install the application**

- **Internet connection**

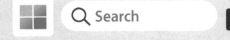

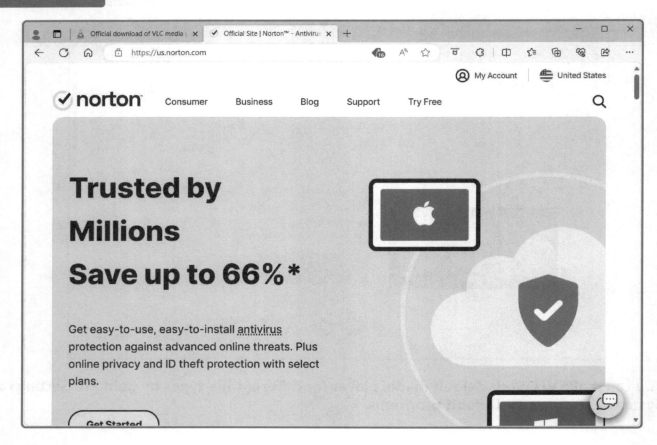

You must acquire a license for this software by using your browser to navigate to **https://it.norton.com/products?inid=support-nav_norton.com-productsoverview.**

Sign up for Norton personal account, then follow the on-screen instructions to download and install the most recent version. Follow the directions after clicking the installation file in your Downloads library.

Click on the file downloaded. Select "Yes" when prompted by the "Do you want to allow this app to change your device?" dialog box. Following installation, Norton will present a box with a number of suggested settings that you can select or deselect before pressing the Apply button.

You will be asked to enter an activation code when you run the program for the first time. This unique string of letters and digits has the following format: xxxxx-xxxxx-xxxxx-xxxxx-xxxxx-x. This code authorizes you to use the item and confirms that you bought it legally. You will be asked for an activation code when using apps other than Norton.

Installing WhatsApp Messenger

WhatsApp is one of the greatest messaging apps for staying in touch with friends and family, and the desktop version syncs with the smartphone version so you can always access your discussions.

Open the Microsoft Store from the taskbar or from the Start menu. **In the Microsoft Store, type 'WhatsApp' into the search field and select "WhatsApp Desktop."** There will be a 'Free' button; click it to download the program. That's all. The app will be ready to use after the download and installation are complete.

How to Setup Zoom

Zoom is a video chat service that enables you to have video conversations with loved ones. Although many programs are similar to it, it is regarded as one of the most effective and user-friendly.

Visit zoom.us/download and click the Download button. After clicking on the installation file in your Downloads folder, you will be asked "Do you want to allow this app to make changes to your device?" Select yes. After a brief setup, Zoom will be installed and ready for use.

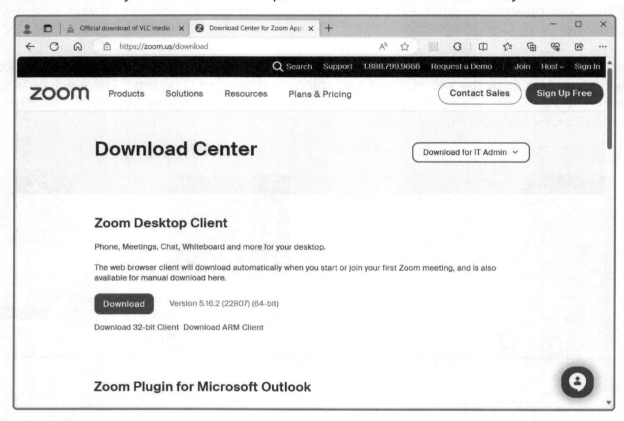

Things to Remember

When installing new software, Windows 11 will always ask you if you wish to enable the app to make changes to your device. Proceed only if the software has been validated and is trusted. You can find out how reliable a program is by doing some preliminary research on the internet.

When installing new software, it is equally vital to read through all requested permissions and avoid agreeing to any needless terms or conditions. Some programs may request permission to access or update your privacy settings, photos and videos, or full network access even though they do not require this information to function properly.

A calendar app, for example, does not require access to your media. Before continuing, make sure to uncheck these items.

Chapter 6:

Backup and Restore:
Keep Your Memories and Documents
Safe (Photos, Videos, Documents)

Our data (photos, documents, contacts, and emails) are among our most valuable assets in the digital age. But what if your computer broke or you misplaced your smartphone? This is why it is critical to perform regular backups of your data. Consider making a photocopy of your most important documents and storing it in a secure location.

Backing up your Data

- **Determine what to save:** First, decide what information you want to keep. Photos, documents, emails, contacts, and other items may be included.

- **Choose where you want to save:** An external hard drive, USB sticks, or cloud storage services such as OneDrive, Google Drive, or Dropbox can all be used.

- **Backup your data:** Many computers have built-in backup programs. Follow the instructions and do it regularly.

How to Restore Data from Backups:

- **Connect your backup storage device:** Connect an external hard drive or USB to your computer if you use one.

- **Use backup software:** Many computers include software that allows you to restore data from a backup.

- **Check your files after the restore is finished to ensure** everything was restored correctly.

Making use of OneDrive for automatic backup:

Microsoft's OneDrive is a cloud storage service that can automatically backup your data. Once configured, it will automatically save your files to the cloud, allowing you to access them from any device, wherever you are.

- **Setup:** Sign in to OneDrive with your Microsoft account and select the folders you want to be automatically backed up (always select the important files you don't want to lose)

- **Work continues as usual:** Once configured, OneDrive will save any new files or changes you make in the background.

- **Access:** You can access your files from any Internet-connected device by logging into your OneDrive account.

Which is better: OneDrive, Google Drive, or Dropbox?

All three of these services are excellent cloud storage options, but which one you select depends on your requirements:

1) **OneDrive:** Is ideal for Windows and Office users due to its tight integration with these platforms. If you frequently use Word, Excel, or PowerPoint, OneDrive could be a good option for you.

2) **Google Drive:** If you frequently use Gmail, Google Photos, or Google Workspace services (such as Docs, Sheets, and Slides), Google Drive provides seamless integration.

3) **Dropbox:** Known for its ease of use and dependability, Dropbox is compatible with nearly all operating systems and devices. It's ideal for sharing files with others, thanks to its simple sharing interface.

OneDrive access and backup

Sign in to OneDrive as follows:

1) **Launching the website:** Launch your browser and navigate to **https://onedrive.live. com.**

2) **Login: A "Sign In"** button can be found in the upper right corner of the page. Click on it.

3) **You can sign in if you already have a Microsoft account** (for example, an Outlook. com or Hotmail.com email address). If you don't already have an account, click "Create Account" and follow the instructions to set one up.

Login has been completed:

After signing in, you'll be taken to your OneDrive home page, where you can view all of your saved files and folders.

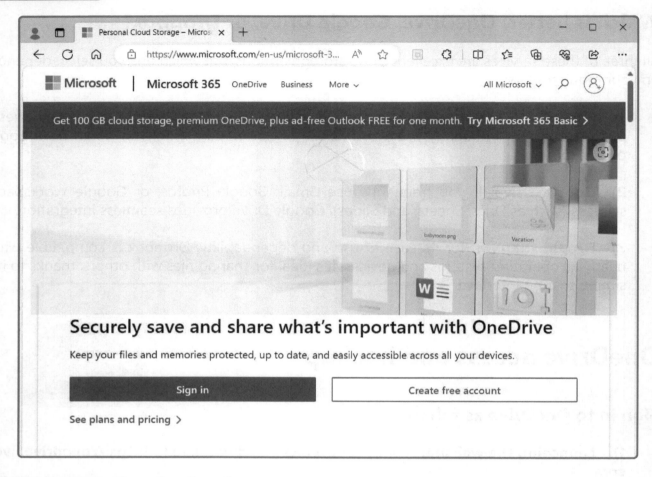

Using OneDrive for backup:

Installing the OneDrive application:

1) **Install the OneDrive app on your device** to back up files from your computer. Navigate to the OneDrive website and download the app for your operating system (Windows, Mac, and so on).

2) **Configuration:** Launch the app after installation and sign in with your Microsoft account.

3) **OneDrive will ask you which folders you want to back up** during the initial setup. It will select folders such as Documents, Pictures, and Desktop by default, but you can change the selection to suit your needs.

4) Backup automatically: Once you've selected your folders, OneDrive will synchronize them with the cloud. OneDrive will automatically sync any files you add or edit in one of these folders.

5) Manual: Drag specific files or folders into the OneDrive folder on your computer if you want to backup only those items that aren't already in your default folders. Following that, these files are synced and uploaded to your cloud storage account.

6) Confirm: Checking your OneDrive app frequently will help you make sure that all of your files are up to date. Your files were successfully synced if you see tiny green checkmarks next to them.

Considerations:

Storage: At the time of my last review in 2022, OneDrive provided limited free storage (5GB). Additional storage plans can be purchased if you require more space.

Internet connection: When syncing files, make sure you have a stable internet connection, especially if you are uploading or downloading large amounts of data.

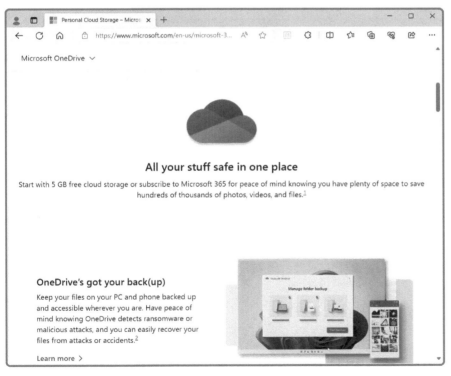

You can have peace of mind knowing that your data is safe in the cloud and accessible from any device with an internet connection if you use OneDrive.

With a few simple steps, you can protect your digital life from accidental loss or device failure.

Chapter 7:

Use Windows 11 for Web Navigation

The primary and most well-known browsers for surfing the internet are Microsoft Edge and Google Chrome

Although both browsers are relatively similar, the next chapter will explain how to use them for some of the most crucial tasks.

Utilizing a Web Browser

Many buttons and features are available on browsers to enhance your online browsing experience.

Navigating Microsoft Edge

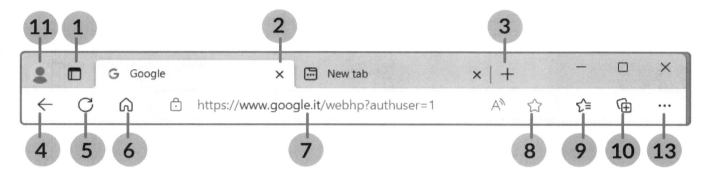

1) The tab actions menu lets you view recently closed tabs and other tab choices.

2) Exit this tab

3) Add New tab

4) Go back

5) Reload the page.

6) Access the homepage

7) The address bar is where you can type in URLs or search queries.

8) Make this page a favorite.

9) See your favorite items.

10) Create reading lists that you can revisit later using the "Add to a collection" function.

11) Access your account and profile details on your user profile.

12) Extra tools

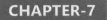

Navigating Google Chrome

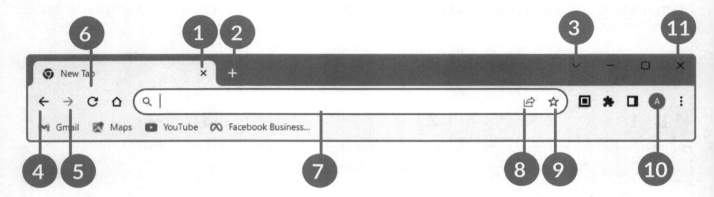

1) Close the active tab

2) Launch a fresh tab

3) View a list of recently opened and closed tabs

4) Go to the previous web page (TIPS: If you hold down the back button, a drop-down menu pops up, and you choose which web page to go to, even 2 or 3 past pages that you visited.)

5) Move ahead

6) Reload the page.

7) The address bar, where you can type URLs or search queries.

8) Share this page - You can make a shareable link, email the page to a connected device, create a QR code, cast the page to a nearby device, or save the page as an HTML file by clicking this link. Additionally, you can share immediately on Twitter, LinkedIn, Facebook, and WhatsApp.

9) Add a bookmaker

10) View your account and profile information in your user profile

11) Extra tools

What do Tabs do?

To open numerous online pages in the same window, internet browsers use Tabs. Your desktop can avoid being cluttered by using tabs. In your browser, tabs are displayed above the address bar at the very top. You can launch a new one quickly by just clicking the + sign to the right of the tab you're now using.

Any link can be opened in a new tab by right-clicking and choosing "Open in new tab." A link can also be opened in a brand-new window by right-clicking and choosing "Open in new window."

Adding a Bookmark

You can return to a website in the future by saving and storing its URL with a bookmark.

Microsoft Edge:

- Visit the website you wish to save the URL for.

- On the toolbar's right side, select the Star button.

- To add a "Favorite," click the star button with the plus symbol.

- The name of your website will now show.

- To save, press Enter.

- To keep your Favorites organized, you can change the website's name or create folders and subfolders.

- You may also rapidly add a website to your Favorites by pressing the keyboard combination Ctrl+D.

Google Chrome

- Visit the website that has the URL you want to save.

- Click on the Star icon on the right side of the toolbar.

- Now, you can choose the folder and website names you want to save.

- Press Enter to save.

- The Ctrl+D keyboard shortcut allows you to add a website to your Bookmarks. Remember that to organize the bookmarks well, you may rename the website's name and make folders and subfolders.

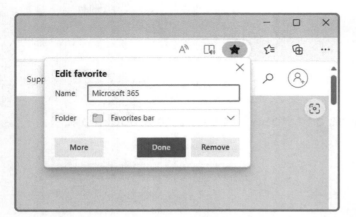

Microsoft Edge

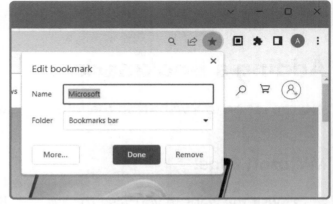

Google Chrome

Method for Displaying the Bookmarks Bar

A bar at the top of your browser can show all of your bookmarks and bookmark folders.

Microsoft Edge

- Select **Settings > Appearance > Customize the toolbar > Show favorites bar** by clicking the Tools button.

- To display the favorites bar, **choose "Always" or "Only on new tabs."**

- The **Ctrl + Shift + B** keyboard shortcut can also be used to rapidly reveal or hide the Favorites bar.

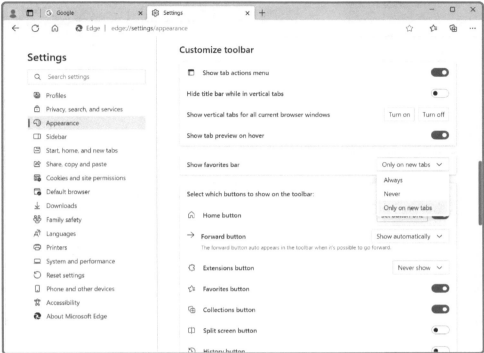

Google Chrome

- Select **Settings > Appearance > Show bookmarks bar** by clicking the Tools button.

- This can be **toggled to show the bookmarks bar.**

- To rapidly reveal or conceal the bookmarks bar, use **Ctrl + Shift + B** on your keyboard.

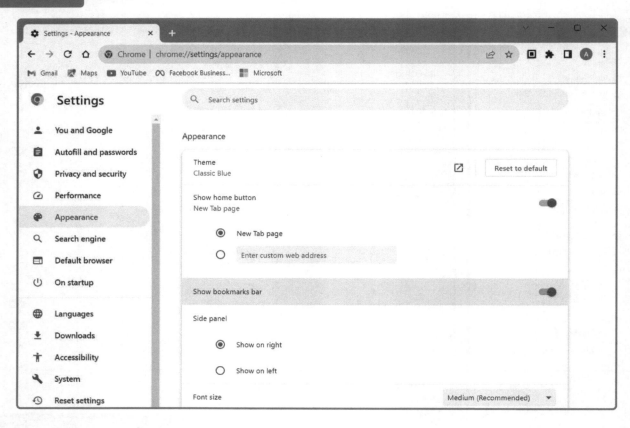

Setting Up a New Homepage

Your browser will open to a default homepage, but you can change it to any website by setting your own homepage.

Google Chrome

- **Open Settings and select Appearance.**

- **Turn "Show Home button" to "on" by clicking the button.**

- Choose whether to make a New Tab Page your homepage or a specific URL.

Microsoft Edge

- **Select Customize toolbar under Settings > Appearance.**

- **Select "Home button" and then choose "Set button URL."**

- You will be taken to the homepage settings from where you can configure your homepage button to open a new tab or a certain URL.

Your Browsing history can be seen and deleted.

Your web browser keeps a log of all the websites you've recently visited. You can quickly browse this data, delete particular records, or clear all the data.

Google Chrome

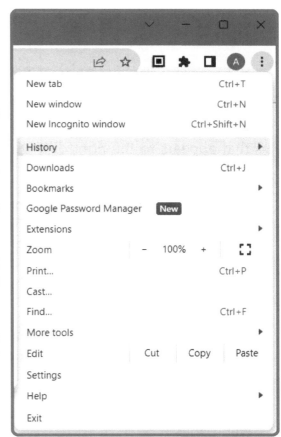

- **Select History by clicking the Tools button.**

- A small window will display some of the websites you have visited in the previous 90 days.

- By clicking on one of these pages, you can view it.

- Open the History tab or **press Ctrl+H to remove the history of your searches.**

- Using the checkboxes, you may pick and deselect specific records. Then, click the Delete button in the top right corner.

- Utilizing the **"Clear browsing data"** option on the left side of the page, **you can erase all of your browser history.**

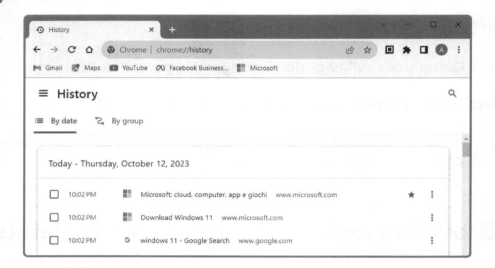

Microsoft Edge

- **By clicking the Tools button, choose History.**

- Some websites you have visited in the last 90 days will be shown in a tiny window.

- Hovering over a record and choosing the X that appears to the right of it will allow you to delete that specific record.

- Click on the three horizontal dots at the top of the History window and select **"Clear browsing data" to remove all of your browser history.**

- You can also view the history of your browser by pressing **Ctrl+H.**

- **Select "Open history page" from the menu that appears after clicking the three horizontal dots at the top of the History window** to view more detailed information, such as the time and date that you viewed your web pages.

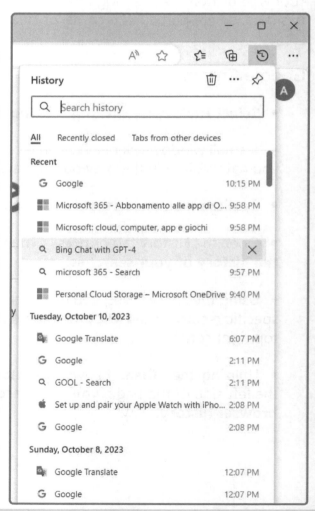

Activating Private Browsing

Your browsing history and other information won't be saved on your device or in your account when you use private browsing. Remember that your internet service provider can still view your network activity even though these modes prevent them from seeing your browsing information.

Microsoft Edge - InPrivate browsing

- Click on the three horizontal dots in the top right corner of your window to launch InPrivate and open a new tab.

- Choosing **"New InPrivate Window."** Alternatively, you can open an InPrivate window by pressing **Ctrl+Shift+N** on your keyboard.

Google Chrome - Incognito Mode

- Click on the three vertical dots in the top right corner of your window to launch an Incognito tab.

- Choose **"New Incognito window."**

- Alternatively, you can launch an Incognito window by pressing **Ctrl + Shift + N** on your keyboard.

Microsoft Edge

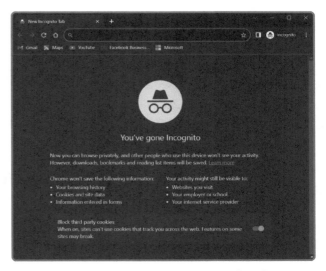

Google Chrome

How to Enlarge a Page

Microsoft Edge

- Click on the three vertical dots in the top right of your browser window.

- **To zoom in or out, select "Zoom" and press + or -.**

- You can also zoom in or out using the mouse wheel while holding down the Ctrl key.

Google Chrome

- Click on the three vertical dots in the top right of your browser window.

- **To zoom in or out, select "Zoom" and press + or -.**

- You can also zoom in or out using the mouse wheel while holding down the Ctrl key.

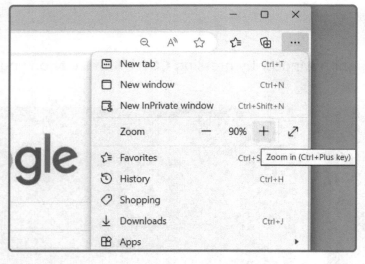 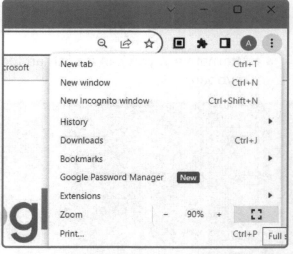

Microsoft Edge   **Google Chrome**

How to Stop Ads from Loading in Your Web Browser

Numerous websites present obtrusive and annoying browser pop-up advertisements. Some of these advertisements can be blocked using your web browser.

Microsoft Edge

- Select **Settings > Cookies and site permissions > Pop-ups and redirects** after clicking the Tools button.

- Be sure to activate this setting.

- Additionally, you can alter these settings to allow or prohibit particular websites from displaying pop-up ads or leading you to alternative pages.

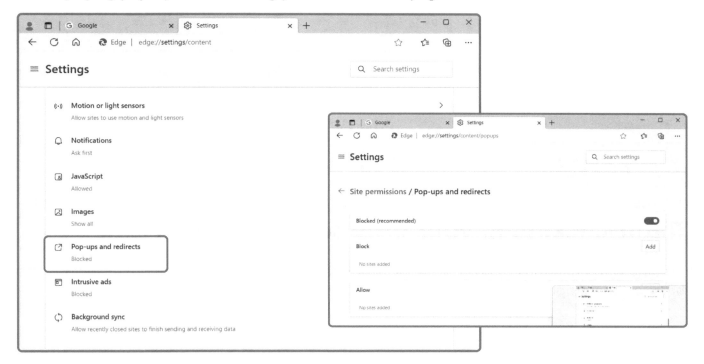

Google Chrome

- To turn off pop-ups and redirects, click the Tools button, then choose **Settings > Security and Privacy > Site settings.**

• Make sure the "Don't allow sites to send pop-ups or use redirects" checkbox is selected under "Default behavior."

• By entering the URLs of the websites you want to allow or prohibit pop-ups from, you can further customize these settings.

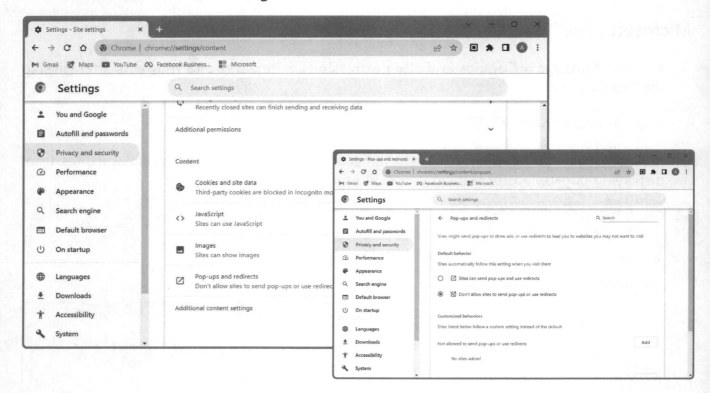

Right-clicking in your browser an image or link

A menu with numerous options will appear when you right-click an image or link in your web browser. These options can help you increase productivity.

Microsoft Edge

• "Open image in a new tab" opens in a new tab with its URL in the address bar.

• By selecting "Save image/link", your File Explorer will open, allowing you to name and select a location on your computer where you want to save the image/link. HTML files are used to store web pages.

• "Copy an image" or a link will put a copy on your clipboard to paste into another program.

• "Copy an image" link will copy its URL to your clipboard.

• "Create a QR Code" for this Image creates a unique QR code that links to the image URL and can be scanned with the camera on your phone.

• "Search the web for images" to find similar ones.

• " Search Bing in the sidebar" opens a sidebar where you can use the Bing search engine to find related pictures.

• "Open in Immersive Reader": This option displays your website in a cleaner, clutter-free layout that enhances reading.

• "Share" lets you send the website link via email, Facebook, or another social media platform.

• To save screenshots, we choose "Web Capture", a clipping tool.

• View the source code of the website by inspecting it.

Google Chrome

• "Open image/link in new tab" - opens the image URL in the address bar of a new tab.

• "Save image/link as" - opens File Explorer and allows you to name and save the image/link to a specific location on your computer. Web pages are saved as HTML files.

• "Copy image/link" - copies the image/link to the clipboard to be pasted into another application.

• "Copy image address" -- copies the image's URL to the clipboard.

- "Create QR Code for this Image" - generates a unique QR code that links to the image URL and can be scanned using the camera on your mobile device.

- "Google Lens" image search - searches the Internet for similar images.

- Inspect the source code of the web page to view it.

How to Download a File

You may want to download content such as a document or an image while browsing the web. Documents are frequently made available for download via a link. You can save these links to your computer by right-clicking and selecting "Save link as...". This will launch your File Explorer, allowing you to name your download and specify where you want the file saved. Similarly, you can save almost any image found online by right-clicking, selecting "Save image as...", naming the image, and specifying a location for saving it.

Extensions and add-ons

Internet browsers provide simple tools for improving and personalizing your browsing experience. Small icons represent these tools to the right of your address bar.

Microsoft Edge

- Add-ons can be accessed by selecting Extensions from the Tools menu. This is also where you will manage your installed extensions.

- You will be redirected to the Edge Add-ons page, where you can search for a variety of tools, including those for accessibility, blogging, communication, developer tools, entertainment, news & weather, photos, productivity, search tools, shopping, social, and sports. This page also includes the categories Most Popular, Newest, Editor's Picks, By Microsoft, and Trending.

- Click the Get button, then select Add Extension from the pop-up window to install an add-on for your web browser. This will add an extension button to the side of your address bar and may redirect you to the developer website for the extension.

- To utilize the add-on, click the small icon next to the address bar and navigate the menu options.

- Verify the ratings for all add-ons, as some may be flawed or ineffective.

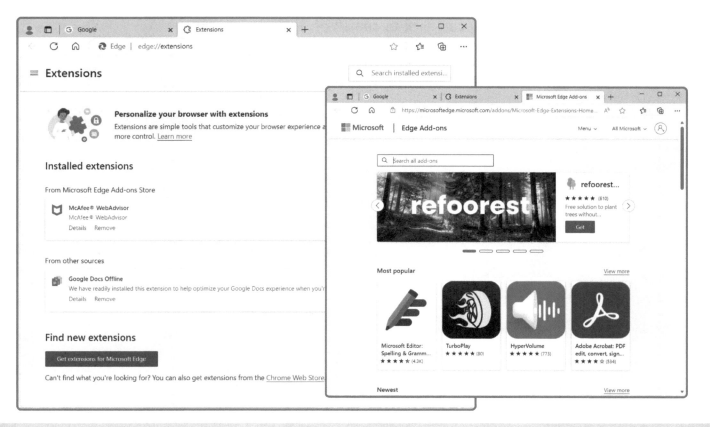

Google Chrome

• Chrome extensions can be found at **chrome.google.com/webstore/category/ extensions. Tools > More tools > Extensions** allows you to manage your existing extensions.

• The link will take you to the Google Web Store, where you can browse thousands of extensions for a variety of purposes such as accessibility, blogging, developer tools, fun, news & weather, photos, productivity, search tools, shopping, social and communication, and sports. The Web Store will also display some featured apps in various categories, such as Recommended for you, Favorites of 2021, Extensions starter kit, Travel smarter, and others.

• To install an extension, right-click it and choose **"Add to Chrome,"** then Add Extension from the pop-up window.

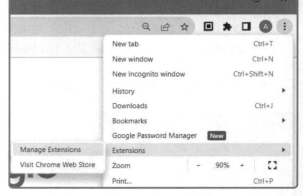

• You should now see a new icon next to your address bar, which you can use to access the extension's features by clicking on it.

• If you don't see a new icon, you should see a puzzle-piece icon that you can click to see all of your extensions. The pin buttons allow you to pin or unpin the extension icons to your taskbar so that they are always visible.

Chapter 8:

Security – Avoid Phishing and Protecting Yourself and Your Data

Understanding and Avoiding Phishing Emails

Digital safety is crucial in the connected world of today. Phishing is a sneaky tactic that is one of the main online threats. The word "phishing" is derived from the verb "to fish," suggesting that the attackers are "fishing" for unwitting victims using false bait.

Knowing the Purpose of Phishing

Phishing is the practice of using carefully crafted emails that impersonate trustworthy organizations to trick people into disclosing sensitive information, such as passwords, credit card numbers, and social security numbers.

Imagine getting an email that appears to be from your bank but is actually malicious.

Important Features of Phishing Emails

- **Request for Personal Information:** Reputable companies do not frequently request personal data via email because they have secure procedures in place. Be cautious if an email requests sensitive information from you.

- **Many phishing attempts can be identified by grammatical and spelling errors: Even though not all phishing emails** contain errors, poor grammar and spelling are frequently a warning sign.

- **Suspicious URLs:** At first glance, the web address included in the email may appear to be legitimate. Hovering over the link, however, frequently reveals a different URL than what the text indicates. Attackers use domains that resemble legitimate ones but have small differences.

- **Phishing emails frequently use scare tactics, like threats of account closures, or make unrealistic promises in order to entice victims.**

- **Unexpected Attachments:** Unwanted emails that include attachments pose a risk. These attachments might include malware such as viruses.

Protection Techniques Against Phishing

- **Always double-check:** If an email seems questionable, get in touch with the business or person in question by phone or email using a confirmed contact method.

- **Use Email Filters:** New email platforms have filtering features that can detect phishing emails and send them to a spam or junk folder.

- **Keep Your Software Updated:** Doing so will guarantee that you have the most recent security patches.

- **Self-education:** Regularly attend webinars or workshops on online security. An effective defense against threats is knowledge.

Increasing Access Through the Use of Password Managers and Strong Passwords

Our main line of defense against unauthorized account access is passwords. Despite being our first line of defense, many people downplay their significance.

Strengthening Your Password:

- **Length and Complexity:** The harder it is to crack your password, the longer and more complex it is. Use a variety of characters, including capital and lowercase letters, symbols, and numbers.

- **Avoid using personal information:** Never use information that is readily available, such as names, birthdays, or anniversaries.

- **Avoid Using Dictionary Words:** Dictionary attacks can be used to break any dictionary-based password, regardless of language.

- **Rotate Passwords:** Changing passwords on a regular basis lowers the likelihood of unauthorized access.

But how are we supposed to remember all these complicated passwords with the numerous accounts that the majority of people have?

Password Managers

Software programs like LastPass, 1Password, and Dashlane not only securely store passwords but also help you create unique, secure passwords. Your online experience is both safe and convenient thanks to their single master password requirement.

Using Two-Factor Authentication (2FA) to Increase Account Security

No matter how secure a password is, it can still be broken. As a second line of defense, two-factor authentication (2FA) makes sure that even if your password is stolen, your account is still secure.

A Simple Explanation of Two-Factor Authentication (2FA)

Consider having a safe in your house. A key is required to open this safe. Imagine that in addition to the key, you are also required to enter a secret code in order to open it. This dual mechanism, with the key and the code, increases the security of your safe.

When you try to log in to your online account, such as an email inbox or a social media profile, two-factor authentication works similarly.

Here's a step-by-step explaination:

First Factor - Something You Are Aware Of: Typically, this is a password. It's similar to the key to your safe. You must enter it each time you want to log into your account.

Second Factor - Owning Something: After entering your password, the system will request additional verification to ensure that you are who you say you are. This proof could be a temporary code sent via SMS to your phone or generated by a special app. This code is similar to the safe's secret code in that it changes every time and is only valid for a limited time.

But why use two-factor authentication?

Assume someone finds the key to your safe. That person could easily open it if I didn't have an additional secret code. However, with the additional code, the safe remains locked and secure even if the key is compromised.

The same is true online. If someone discovers or guesses your password (your "key"), they will be unable to access your account unless they have the 2FA code (the "secret code").

How to Configure 2FA:

1) Security Settings page: Access your online account by logging in, then choose the privacy or security settings.

2) Platforms will offer the option to enable 2FA (note: the platform or website will automatically ask you if you want to activate two-factor authentication if the site provides this type of security.)

3) Pick an authentication method: This could be an email, a text message to your phone, or an app like Google Authenticator.

4) Finish the setup: obey the directions displayed on the screen. To make sure the code was properly received, the majority of services will require you to enter it.

**5) The slight inconvenience of entering a second code significantly increases the security of your account.

Chapter 9:

Getting in touch with Microsoft Teams

Microsoft Teams is the company's flagship video chat and instant messenger service, allowing you to chat with your contacts and make one-on-one or group video calls.

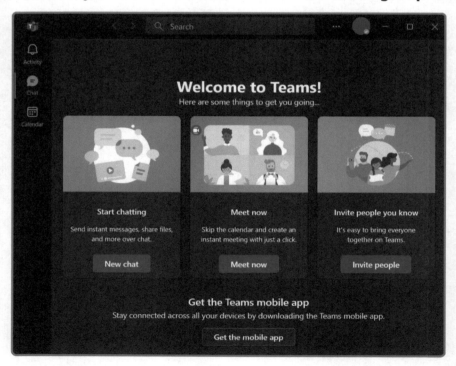

Many useful features are included, such as screen sharing, scheduling, messaging, and the ability to record video chats. It's a fantastic app for staying in touch with friends and family all over the world.

Teams has been split into two apps: Chat and Teams. Both will be included with your operating system.

The Chat app will only appear as a simple pop-up window with a chat interface. Launch the Teams app to access all of the features. The standard versions are only for personal use, and some advanced features may be missing. To gain access to these features, you must purchase the Business or School versions.

Configuring Microsoft Teams

The Chat icon can be found here. You should be able to find the app in your taskbar or by searching 'Chat' in the Start menu. If you can't find Chat, you can get it from the Microsoft Store.

You can also download Microsoft Teams onto your Android or iOS device via the Google Play Store or the Apple App Store to make connecting easier.

Sign-In and Start-Up

- Click the Chat app icon in the taskbar or Start Menu

- When you first use the app, you will be prompted to create an account. Sign in to your Windows 11 device with your Microsoft account.

- The Chat app will then request your smartphone's phone number. Make certain to enter the correct country code.

- This number will receive a two-step verification code. Confirm the code by pressing the next button.

- All of your contacts will be synced by the Chat app.

- To launch the full version of Teams, type 'teams' into the Start menu and click the icon.

Begin a New Conversation

- Click the Chat icon on the left side of the app window in Teams.

- Fill in the 'To:' section at the top of the screen with your contact's name, email, or phone number.

- You can also start a conversation with one of your groups.

- Begin typing your message near the bottom of the app window.

- Attachments, GIFs, and other types of fun graphics can be easily added to your messages.

- To send your message, click the small arrow icon in the bottom right corner.

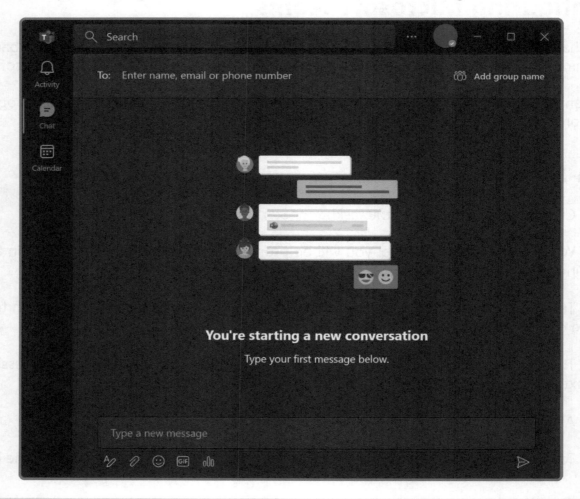

Begin a Video Chat

- To start a video call, click the Chat icon on the left side of the application.

- Select "Start new meeting."

- Give the group a name. Any identifying name that informs your contacts of what to anticipate when they accept your invitation can serve as this.

- Select "Get a link to share" to generate a URL you can send to any of your contacts. By clicking on this link, they can attend your meeting.

- Alternatively, you can choose "Start meeting," which will launch a video chat and let you manually add participants.

- Before starting your meeting, make sure your camera and microphone are set up correctly and prepared for use.

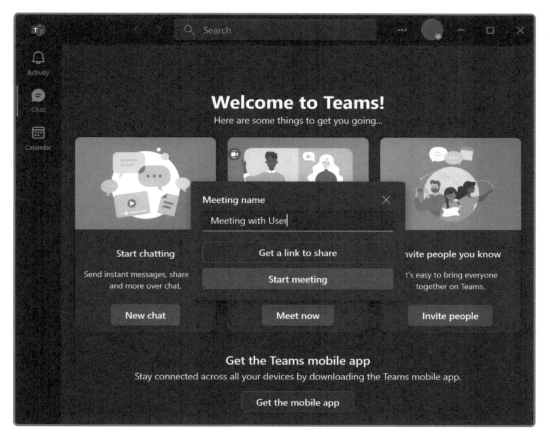

Meeting Management

- Once in a meeting, you will see all participants displayed, with each person in their own tile, and the name of the meeting displayed in the title bar at the top of the window.

- A toolbar with the following buttons runs across the top of the window:

  ○ The length of your meeting

  ○ The Teams icon - click to see the names of all meeting participants.

  ○ The Chat icon - click to open a chat window with all meeting participants.

  ○ A "Raise your hand" icon - click to notify meeting participants that you wish to speak. When someone else presses this button, a yellow box will appear around their tile.

- The three-dots button provides access to additional settings:

  ○ Device settings

o   Meeting options

o   Meeting notes

o   Meeting details

o   Gallery/large gallery/together mode - use these modes to modify how you view the tiles of the meeting participants. You can view numerous small tiles, fewer large tiles, the active speaker alone, etc.

o   Fullscreen or Focus mode.

o   Background effects such as solid colors, File Explorer images, and animated backgrounds.

o   In the business version, you'll also find the recording button here.

a) A button for turning the camera on and off.

b) A button to enable or disable the microphone.

c) A screen sharing button that allows others to view your screen.

d) The Leave button, which ends or exits a meeting.

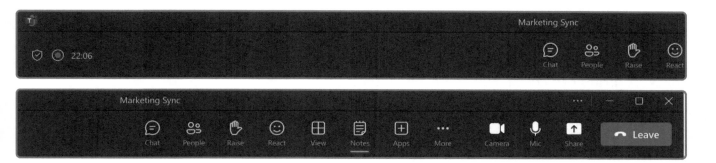

Invite Contacts

• Add your contacts to the Teams app so you can quickly start conversations or meetings with them by typing just their name instead of searching for their email address or phone number.

- In the app, click the Chat icon on the left and then choose "Invite people."

- You can enter your contacts' names, email addresses, phone numbers, and any other necessary details when adding them.

Create a New Group

- Utilize groups to make it simple to communicate with various subsets of your contacts. You could create a group for your grandchildren, one side of your family, your coworkers with whom you are collaborating on a particular project, and more.

- To create a group, select the Chat icon on the app's left side.

- A drop-down menu will appear at the top of the screen; select "Contacts."

- Next, select "Create a new contact group" from the page's bottom menu.

- Give the group a name and include all of your contacts.

- Instead of adding each person one at a time, the group can now be talked to or video chatted with.

- A group can contain up to 64 individuals.

Using Teams and the Calendar App

- Make reservations for meetings using the integrated Calendar app.

- On the Teams app's left side, select Calendar.

- To set up your meeting, click the desired day and time.

- Next, perform a right-click on the calendar or select "+ New meeting" from the purple button.

- Give your video chat a name, then invite every contact you want to participate.

- Before saving, double check that the date and time are accurate.

Settings

- By selecting the three-dot icon in the top right corner of the window, which is located next to your profile picture, you can access Team app settings.

- You'll see a settings window that includes:

  ○ **General** - Change your language, time zone, and date format preferences in the General section. You can also choose to have Teams launch automatically.

  ○ **Notifications** - You can customize your notifications by setting alerts for particular contacts or activities, muting alerts, setting your notification sounds for incoming

messages or video chat requests, and changing how notifications appear on your screen.

o **Appearance and accessibility** - Choose from Light, Dark, or High contrast themes, and enable or disable animations.

o **People** - Manage your contacts and modify each person's permissions.

o **Privacy** - Change the privacy settings for Teams to either public or private to let others see your activity or to require a link before they can join a chat or video call.

o **Plans and upgrades** - By upgrading your subscription plan and entering your monthly or yearly billing payment information, you can access Teams for Business or Schools.

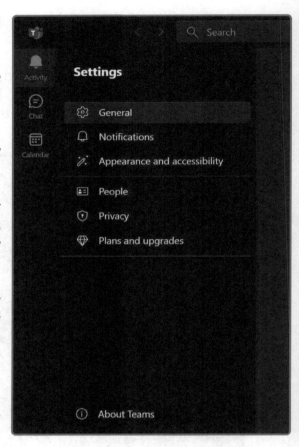

Chat application

• Click the Chat icon in your taskbar to launch the condensed and simplified version of Teams.

• A small pop-up window will appear, displaying your most recent chats and synced contacts.

• To start a new meeting, click the 'Meet' button at the top of the window.

• To start a new chat, click the "Chat" button at the top of the window.

• To launch the full version of the Teams app, click the "Open Microsoft Teams" button at the bottom of this window.

Chapter 10:

Emailing Your Friends and Family

Email has changed a lot since its early days. Now, you can use apps or a web browser to check your email in many different ways. For instant messaging, use the Mail app or another email client.

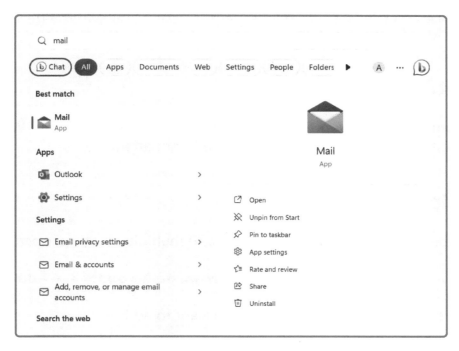

Native Windows 11 Mail App

How to Create a New Email Account

- Using the Start menu, launch the Mail application.

- Choose Add account if this is your first time using the app.

- If you have previously used the app, you must select Manage Accounts under Settings in the navigation pane on the left.

- Choose the type of account you want to create. You have the option of using an already-existing Outlook account or making a new one. You can also use a Google, Yahoo, Office 365, or an iCloud account. You can also use POP or IMAP-based email accounts, but this will require more complex setup procedures.

- You must enter the special 2-step verification code sent to your email or phone number if you choose a Google account and have enabled two-step verification (recommended).

- Enter the login information, which includes the password and email address.

- After clicking Done, your account will start syncing. Your entire email and contact database will be downloaded by the mail app.

Advanced Setup

Older email accounts may necessitate more advanced configuration options. When prompted, select Advanced options and then enter the required information.

Adding Multiple Email Addresses

You can add multiple accounts to the Mail app.. To add multiple accounts, open the Mail app:

1) In the navigation pane, select **Settings > Manage Accounts > + Add Account.**

2) From the list, select the email account you want to add.

3) Configure your account by following the same steps as before.

4) By selecting your account from the navigation pane, you can access mail from multiple accounts.

5) When creating new emails, ensure that they are sent from the correct email account. To switch accounts, click on the desired email address in the navigation pane.

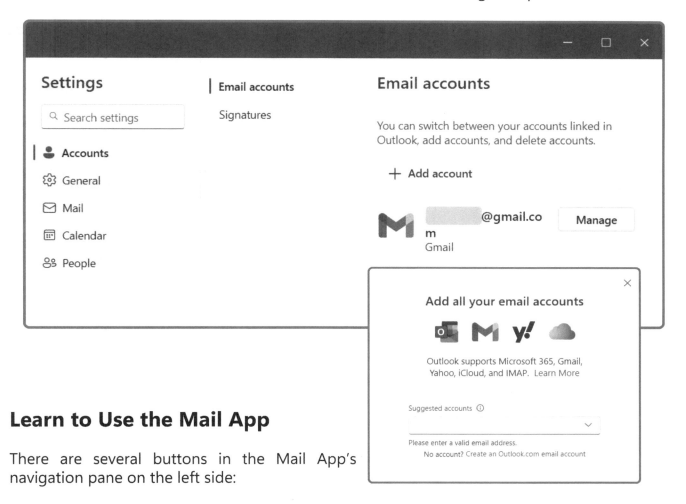

Learn to Use the Mail App

There are several buttons in the Mail App's navigation pane on the left side:

1) **Collapse** - reduces clutter by collapsing the navigation pane.

2) **+ New mail -** creates a new email.

3) **Accounts** - View information about your account.

4) **Folders** - This category includes your Inbox, Drafts, Sent, and Archive folders.

5) Switch to Mail - Switches between the Mail and Calendar apps.

6) **Toggle between the Mail and Calendar apps** with Switch to Calendar.

7) **Settings** enables you to access the Mail App's settings.

In the messaging list pane, you'll notice a search bar, a refresh button, and a selection mode button. You can search for specific terms or keywords in your emails using the search bar.

The refresh button will cause all incoming and outgoing mails to be downloaded and uploaded.

The selection mode allows you to choose which emails to delete or move to a different folder. Finally, on the right side of the window is the reading/writing pane.

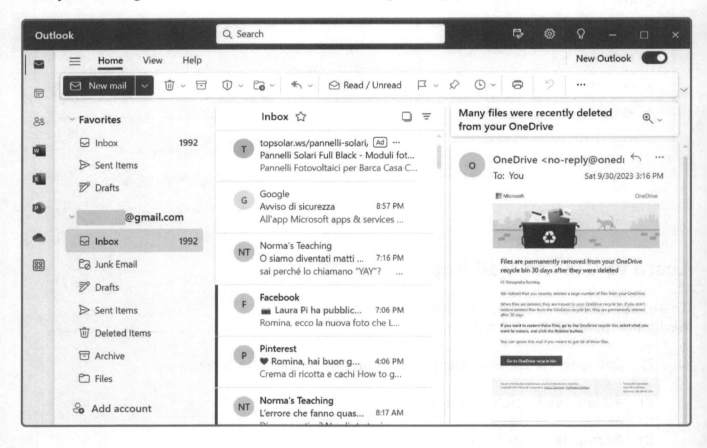

Compose your First Email

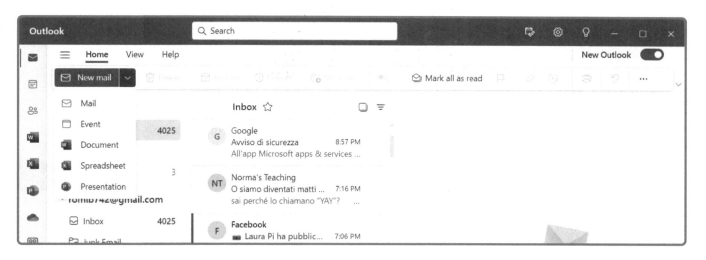

• Click the **+ New Mail button** in the navigation pane to open a new writing pane on the right side of the window.

    ○   In the 'To:' section, enter your recipient's email address.

    ○   You can send an email to multiple people at the same time by entering their email addresses here. The other email addresses you've included will be visible to your recipients.

    ○   You can also add people to your email's CC list. CC stands for "carbon copy," and you can use it to send a copy of an email to someone who is not the primary recipient. When sending work emails, the CC feature comes in handy: you can send something to a colleague and CC your manager to keep track of all communications.

• In the Subject line, type a title for your email.

• Fill in the text field with your email address.

    ○   Many options are available at the top of the writing pane, including Format, Insert, Draw, and Options.

    ○   Text formatting tools such as Bold, Italics, Underline, Bullet lists, and Styles are available in Format.

    ○   Insert lets you add files, tables, images, or links to your email.

o With the Draw tools, you can add freehand notes or doodles to your email. Text can also be highlighted or circled.

o The Options tab provides spell checking tools, zoom and find tools, and the ability to mark your emails as high or low priority.

- When you've finished writing your email, press the Send button.

- You can delete anything in your email by clicking the Delete button.

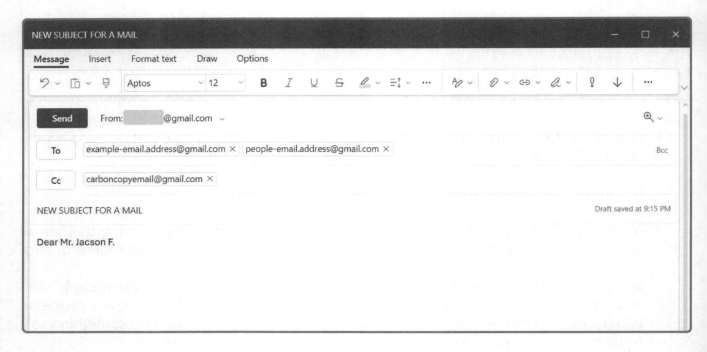

How to Attach Files to an Email

You can easily attach files, pictures, tables, and links to emails using the Mail app's Insert tab. However, you can drag and drop files and other media from File Explorer onto your message draft to attach them to the email.

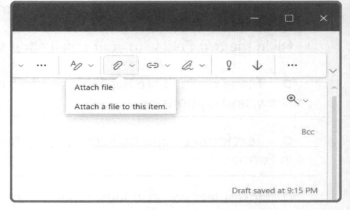

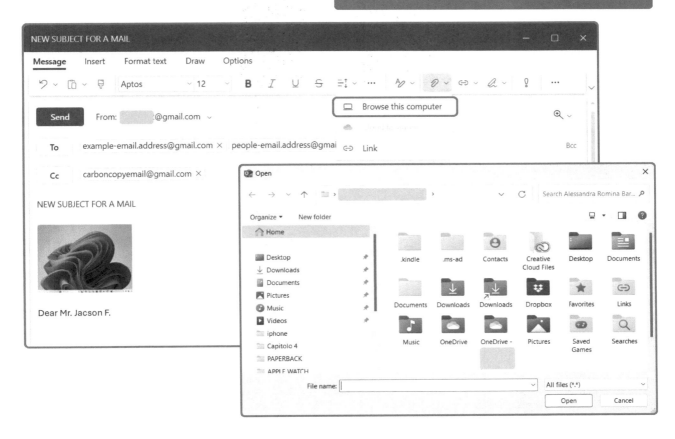

Email Reading and Replying

- To check for new messages, press the refresh button at the top of your Mail app.

- If there are new emails to read, you will see a number next to your Inbox or other relevant folders. Select the folder by clicking on it.

- Your messages will be displayed in the messaging list pane, with unread messages highlighted in bold text to make them easier to find.

- To view the unread email, click on it in the reading pane on the right.

- To respond, click the **'Reply'** button at the top of the window.

- You can also select "Reply all" to send a response to everyone who received the original email.

- Forward is used to send a copy of the email as well as your response to a different email address.

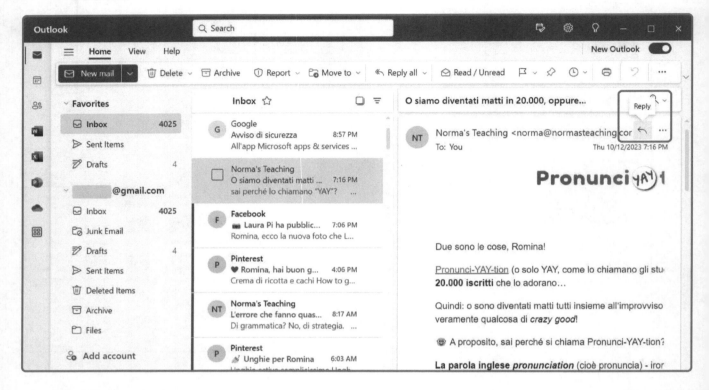

- You can archive your email, which means it will be removed from the Inbox but saved in the Mail app for future access, and you can also delete any emails you receive.

- Other options are available via the Tools button on the top right-hand side of the preview pane:

    - **Set flag** - assign a priority to the email.

    - **Mark as unread**

    - **Move to a different folder.**

    - **Move to the spam folder.**

    - **View the previous mail** or the next mail in your Inbox.

    - **Find a word or phrase** in your email.

- **Save as to store the mail in a text format.**

- **Print**

- **Zoom**

You can open any email in a new window and view multiple windows at the same time. Double-click on the email in your inbox folder to do so.

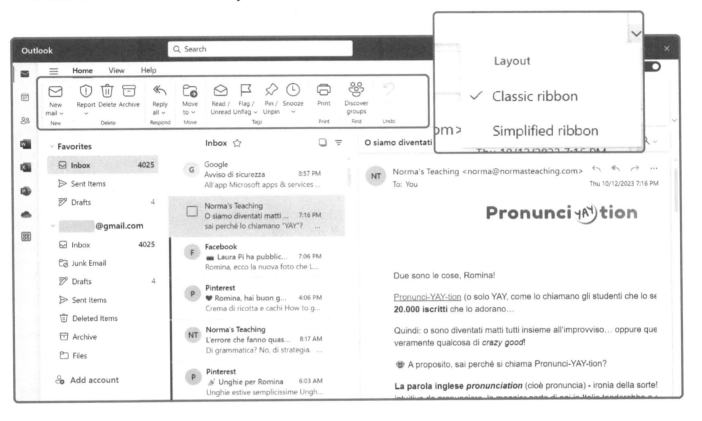

What is the Spam Folder

The spam folder is a useful feature that assists you in keeping your Inbox free of junk, clutter, advertisements, and other forms of unwanted solicitation. All incoming emails are automatically filtered for spam and routed to the spam folder by the Mail app. The Mail app searches for spoofed or unverifiable email addresses, blank messages, phishing scams, and mail that appears to be spam. Every 30 days, the spam folder will be cleared.

If you receive spam in your Inbox, you can mark it as spam by clicking on the Tools icon in the upper right corner of the window and selecting 'Mark as spam,' which will help improve the Mail app's filters in the future.

Making Folders and Sorting Mail

By default, your email will be organized into different folders. The primary folders are as follows:

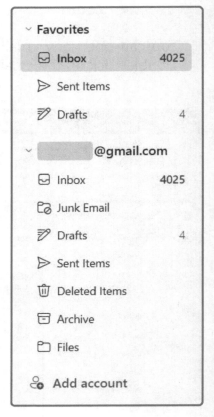

- **Inbox** - This is where you will find all of your primary emails.

- **Drafts** - Here you will find emails that you have started but have not yet sent.

- **Sent items -** this is where you'll find any emails you've sent.

- **Archive** - Here you will find archived items.

- **Deleted Items** - For a limited time, the Mail app will save deleted emails so that you can restore them if necessary.

- **Junk Email** - For a limited time, your junk and spam emails are stored here.

Create more personalized folders such as Work, Personal, Friends, Family, and so on to sort and organize your emails.

To make a new folder, **right-click** anywhere in the navigation pane and choose **"Create new folder."** Subfolders can also be created by **right-clicking an existing folder and selecting "Create new subfolder."** For example, you could have a Work folder with subfolders such as Boss, Colleagues, Clients, and so on.

Drag and drop your folders into place to arrange and sort them in order of importance. **Specific folders can also be marked as Favorites by right-clicking and selecting "Add to Favorites."** Your Favorite folders are pinned near the top of the Folders section in the navigation pane,

making them always accessible and eliminating the need to scroll to find them.

Folders contain a plethora of other useful tools. When you right-click on a folder, you can rename, delete, or move it to a new location.

You can empty a folder or mark all of the emails contained within as read. You can also pin a folder to your Start menu for quick access to your important emails.

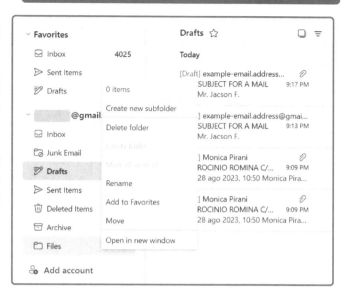

Customizing Your Mail App

Many aspects of the Mail app's appearance and behavior are customizable:

- Personalize the messaging list pane by changing swipe actions, organization, preview text, sender pictures, and image previews in **Settings**.

- Personalize the reading pane by changing the settings for auto-open, mark item as read, caret browsing, and external content.

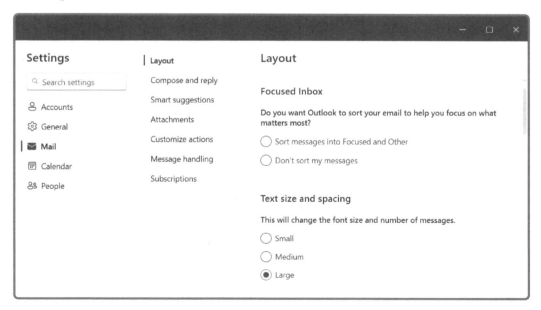

- To sign off on your emails, **create a personalized email signature.**

- Customize your email notifications by pinning sounds, banners, and folders to the Start menu.

- Change the background image, folder color, and message spacing, or go dark.

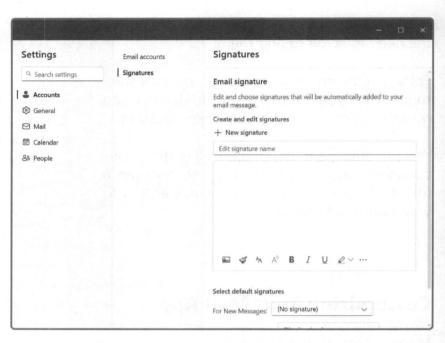

Google Mail (Gmail)

Google Mail is a great alternative to the Mail app, but it only works with 'Gmail' email addresses.

- To access Google Mail, go to **www.gmail.com.**

- To log in, enter your Gmail email address and password.

The Gmail web page looks similar to the Windows 11 Mail app, with a navigation pane on the left that allows you to access all of your folders. Google Meet, a video conferencing service, and Google Hangouts, a cross-platform messaging service, are also available.

Your emails are displayed in the center of the web page. Unread emails and folders containing unread emails will be bolded. To view the entire message, click on the emails.

You can quickly sort through your emails by selecting or deselecting to delete, mark as read, or move emails to a different folder using the checkboxes on the right of each email.

Google Mail Email Composition

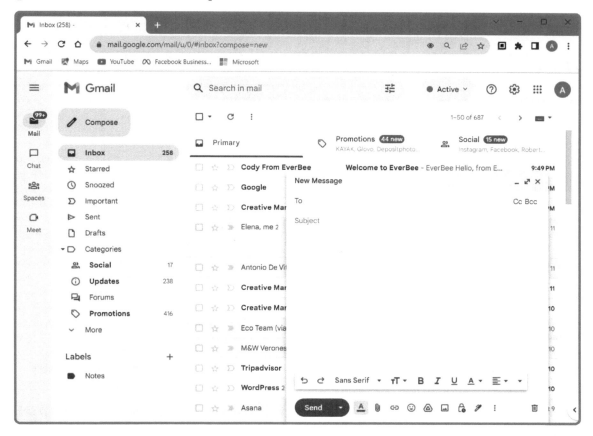

To start a new email, click the Compose button in the upper left corner of the screen.

- A small window will appear in the bottom right corner of the screen. You can enter your recipient's email address here, as well as CC or BCC other contacts and define the subject line.

- The toolbar at the bottom of this window provides several options:

- Attach a file with File Explorer

- Insert a link

- Insert an emoji

- Insert a file with Google Drive

- Insert a photo,

- Toggle confidential mode on or off

- Add a signature

- You can also choose to send your message at a later time by clicking the small arrow next to the Send button.

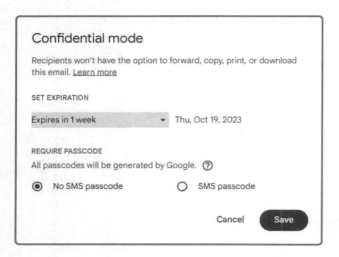

Google Mail Preferences

The quick settings menu provides numerous options for customizing the appearance of the web page, such as layout, theme, inbox type, and reading pane positioning. More settings are available by clicking the "See all settings" button at the top of the quick settings.

This will open a new window where you can access General, Labels, Inbox, Accounts and Import, Filters and Blocked addresses, Forwarding and POP/IMAP, Add-ons, Chat and Meet, Advanced, Offline, and Theme settings.

Chapter 11:

Applications for Your Daily Life

You can use a variety of tools available in Windows 11 to increase your productivity and make your daily tasks simpler and more effective. These apps are available in the Microsoft Store.

Microsoft Apps
Calendar

Windows 11 includes the Calendar app as standard software. By selecting the time and date icon located to the right of your taskbar, you can quickly see it. Click the Calendar app icon in the Start menu or on your taskbar to launch it and view all of its features.

You can switch between and share data from each app thanks to the connection between the Calendar app and the Mail, People, and To Do apps. Each of these apps' icons can be found at the bottom of the navigation pane.

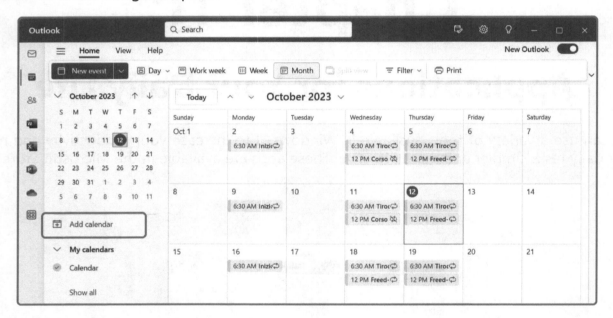

Add an Account

- The Calendar app needs to be connected to an email account, such as your Google or Microsoft account.

- Click **Settings > Manage accounts > Add account** to add a new account. Enter your password and email address. Your account information will sync with the Calendar app if you grant any permissions.

- Using these steps, you can add multiple accounts.

Managing Calendars

• The app allows you to add a wide variety of calendars, including custom calendars, birthdays, holidays, and contacts.

• Click **"Add calendars"** at the bottom of the navigation pane to add a new calendar. Select the kind of calendar you want to include.

• By checking or unchecking the boxes to the left of a calendar's name, you can display or hide calendars to clear up space.

• You can delete calendars by right-clicking and choosing "Remove calendar."

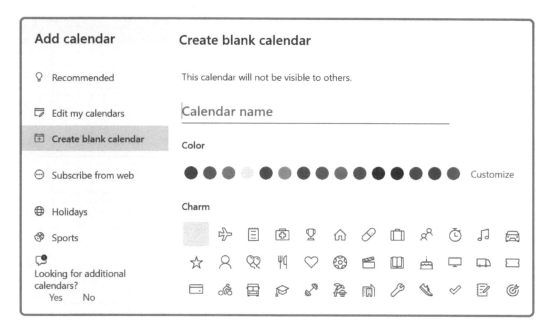

Create an Event

You can create a variety of events in the Calendar app, including:

Quick Event

• Open the Calendar app and select the day you want to schedule the event to create a Quick Event.

• You can enter the event name, time, location, and reminder information in a small pop-up window that will appear.

• Events are by default set to "Add day". By clicking the gray circle to the left of the event name, you can also set an icon or emoji in addition to unchecking this box and setting the start and end times.

• By clicking the title bar at the top of this pop-up and choosing the appropriate account from the drop-down menu, you can modify which account or calendar the event will be associated with.

• To add this event to your calendar, click 'Save'.

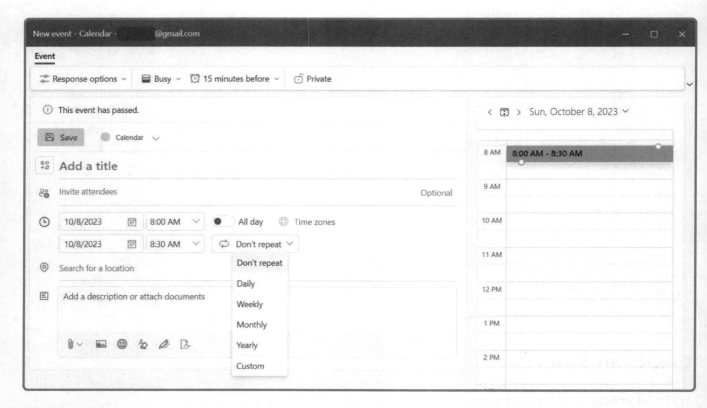

Detailed Event

• Click "More details" from the Quick Event pop-up's bottom menu or "New event" at the top of the navigation pane to add a Detailed Event.

• In the newly opened pane, enter the event name, icon, and desired calendar.

- Set the event venue. You can get directions by finding similar locations with the app.

- To add notes, use the text box at the bottom of the page.

- Users can save, delete, schedule online meetings, set status, set reminders, and repeat events using the top toolbar.

- Use the contact list on the right to invite people to your event.

- Click the 'Save' button to add the event to the calendar.

Group Event

- By including contacts to a detailed event, you can create a group event. The event will be added to the contacts' calendars and they will be notified about it.

- Instead of selecting "Save," click "Send." This will send invitations to all of your contacts, who can accept or reject them.

Repeating Event

- By choosing "New event" and then clicking the "Repeat" button on the toolbar to the right of the window's toolbar, you can create repeating events. This is for recurring events like birthdays, anniversaries, weekly workouts, and other similar occasions.

- Choose daily, weekly, monthly, or yearly repetitions to set the repeat cycle. You can decide to repeat the action daily, twice daily, three times daily, etc. A few additional options can be set here to customize the repeat event exactly how you need it.

- If no end date is specified, the event will continue to occur indefinitely.

- To add the event to your calendar, click 'Save'.

Sharing a Calendar

Your contacts can view or edit the events on calendars that you can share with them.

- To share a calendar, right-click on it in the navigation pane and choose "Share calendar."

- Then press Enter after entering your contacts' email addresses.

- You can select from a drop-down menu whether that contact can edit the event or can only view it.

- To finish, click 'Share'.

Microsoft To Do

A task management tool that functions as a to-do list, Microsoft To Do helps you keep track of all the things you need to get done and lets you check them off as you go.

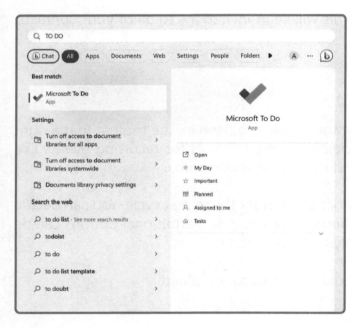

In order to access your lists while traveling, you can sync the To Do app with your smartphone.

In Windows 11, the To Do app is a standard feature:

- To Do can be accessed by typing "to do" into the Start menu.

- When you use the app for the first time, sign in with your Microsoft account.

- To add the app to the taskbar for quick access, select "Yes."

- The app will launch with a focus pane on the right and a navigation pane on the left.

- You can find your account, a search bar, My Day, Important, Planned, Assigned to me, Tasks, Getting started, and lists like Groceries: Buy Now and Buy Later in the navigation pane.

  o All assignments are due today.

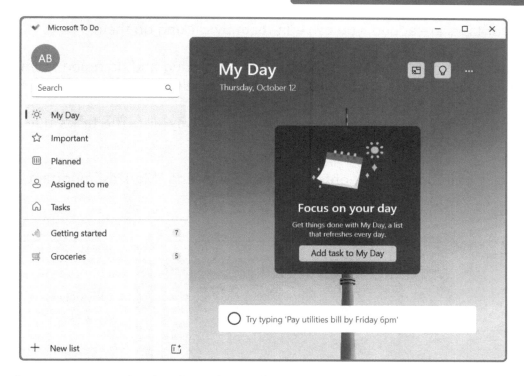

o **Important** - tasks that have been designated as such.

o **Planned** - assignments with approaching deadlines.

o **Assigned** – tasks that have been given to you via the Planner app.

o **Tasks** - Unrelated tasks.

  o One type of smart list is groceries.

Developing a Task

- Choose one of the categories, lists, or groups by clicking on Tasks.

- **Write your task by selecting "Add a task" from the task tab's bottom.**

- To set a due date, a reminder, or a repeat event, use the icons to the right.

- To save the task, hit Enter.

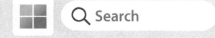 

- Once your tasks are added, you can edit them by clicking on them.

- Drag tasks from one list or group to another by clicking and dragging them. To select a different list, you can also right-click on a task and select "Move task to..."

- Use the right-click menu to add a task to the "My Day" list. The task's due date will be changed to the present day with this action.

- Mark a task as important by right-clicking and selecting "Mark as important."

Subtasks

- When a task has numerous steps that you need to keep in mind, you can add subtasks. You can add a step for each of the materials you require, for instance, if your task is to get craft supplies.

- To add more steps, select "Add Steps," enter the step, and then click "Add Steps."

Add an Attachment

- You are able to attach any type of file to your tasks, including spreadsheets, images, documents, and scans.

- To launch File Explorer, click on your Task and choose **"Add file"**.

- Press Enter after choosing the file you want to attach.

Add Notes

- You can also add more thorough notes to each task to further explain what needs to be done.

- To add a note, click your Task and choose "Add note" to type a succinct description.

Delete Tasks

- To delete a task, select it, and then click the trash can icon in the bottom right corner.

Completing Tasks

- **Click on the circle to the left of a task's name to mark it as completed.**

- Tasks that have been completed will be marked as complete and moved to the bottom of the task pane in a new list titled "Completed."

- Although it is not displayed in the navigation pane, you can enable the Completed list feature:

- Click on "Your Account" in the navigation pane at the top. then click Completed under **Settings > Smart list**. To enable Completed lists in the navigation pane, click the toggle. You can uncheck the circle to mark a task as incomplete.

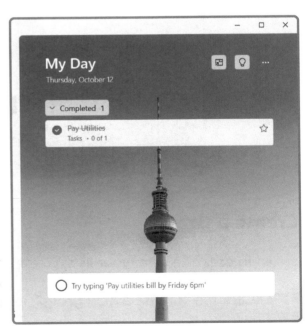

Create a List

- To keep everything organized, you can make several lists. There will be lists displayed in the navigation pane.

- By selecting **"New list"** from the navigation pane's bottom menu, you can make a new list.

- Choose a name for your list, then press Enter.

- Click **"Add a task"** in the task pane to start adding tasks to the list.

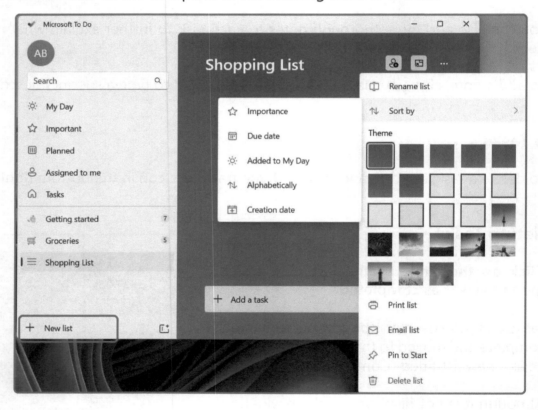

Create a Group

- To organize all of your lists, create groups.

- Click the **"Create a new group"** icon in the navigation pane's bottom right corner to start a new group.

- By selecting **"New list"** from the context menu when you right-click, you can add new lists to this group.

Organizing Tasks, Lists, and Groups

- By selecting the tools icon (three dots) in the task pane's upper right corner, you can sort the tasks in each list.

- You can sort tasks by Creation Date, Importance, Due Date, Added to My Day, or any other column.

List Tools

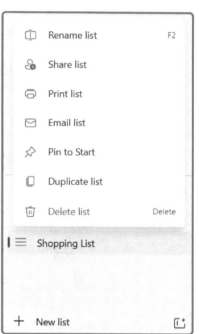

- To access options like **Rename list, Share list, Move list to, Print list, Email list, Pin to Start, Duplicate list, or Delete list, simply right-click on a list in the navigation pane.**

- By right-clicking the list, choosing "Rename," and then clicking the list-icon, you can change it to an emoji or other symbol. Emojis will appear for you to choose from when you do this.

Shortcuts for To Do App

- **Add a task - Ctrl+N**

- **Create a new list - Ctrl+L**

- **Add a task to My Day - Ctrl+T**

- **Complete a task - Ctrl+D**

- **Search - Ctrl+F**

- **Sync - Ctrl+R**

- **Print - Ctrl+P**

Windows Maps App

The Maps app lets you search, explore, and navigate. It can give you driving, walking, or public transportation directions, check traffic and congestion, mark your parking spot, research local businesses, and explore the world in 3D or 360-degree panoramas with Streetside views.

Using Maps

- If you are you are online, the Maps app will display a map with your current location on it.

- Drag the map by clicking and holding to view various regions.

- The map's right sidebar offers a variety of tools, including the ability to zoom in or out and change the map's orientation and imagery.

Search

- By entering a keyword or address in the search bar at the top left of the window, you can find various locations using the Map app.

- You can find the name of the place, its street address, and a description in the search results.

Navigation

- To make your commute quick and simple, you can click on the **'Directions'** button to get turn-by-turn directions from your current location as well as traffic information.

- Maps also make it simple to plan trips by highlighting nearby attractions like dining establishments, shops, hotels, or banks.

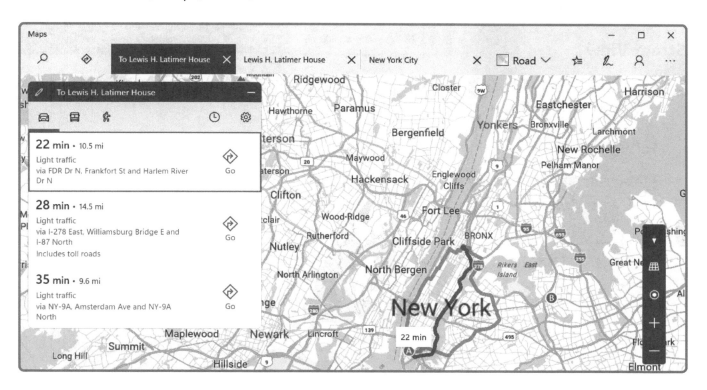

Favorites

- **You can mark a variety of places as favorites.** These will be saved in the Maps application so you can access them later.

- You must look for a location in order to add it as a favorite.

- Choose the appropriate response, then **click the star icon** next to the address.

- Give your favorite places a nickname.

- Near the Search and Direction icons at the top of the window are your favorite items.

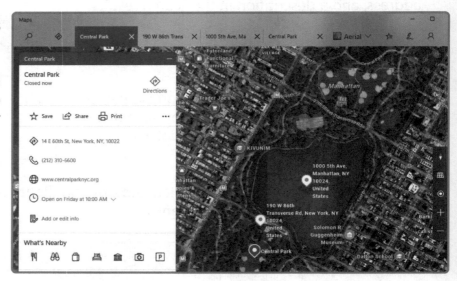

Street View

- Click on the Map views button in the sidebar on the right side of the map to see a 360-degree view of a street.

- Activate the Streetside function.

- You can now choose any place on the map that is highlighted in blue.

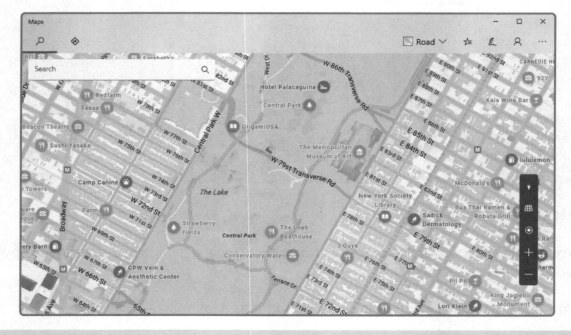

- Additionally, you can use the search function and select the Streetside icon to look up a specific location.

- You will enter Street View mode after doing this. By dragging in any direction or clicking the on-screen arrows, you can move around on the street.

Sticky Notes

You can make digital post-it notes that you can stick to your desktop using the Sticky Notes app. They can be used to store brief notes, inspirational sayings, recollections, or to-do lists.

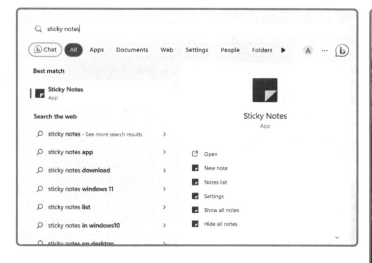

- By typing "sticky notes" into the Start menu, you can access the Sticky Notes app, which will open in a window with a simple interface and few buttons.

- You can switch from light to dark mode by using the settings menu, which also includes color settings, general settings, and sign-in options.

- To securely save your sticky notes, you should sign into your Microsoft account.

Create a New Sticky Note

- A yellow sticky note will show up on the side of the app window when you click the + icon in the top right corner of the window.

- Use the basic formatting tools to edit your note or add a picture after typing it.

- A summary of your sticky note will be visible in the app's main window.

- To change the yellow sticky note's color or remove it, click on the Settings icon (three dots) on the note.

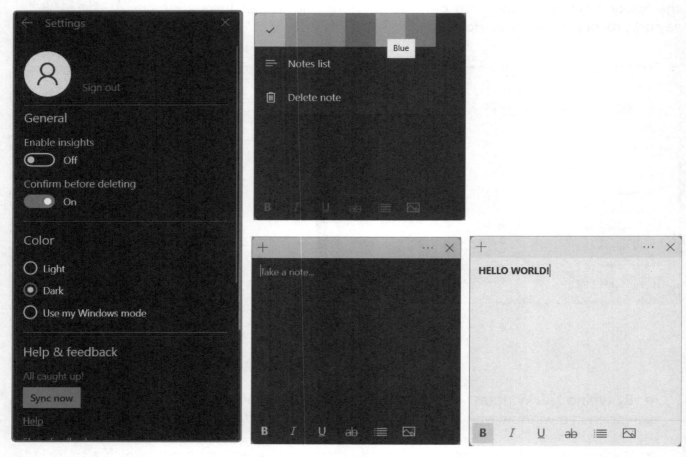

- Sticky notes you've created will continue to be accessible after the app window is closed.

Sticky notes can be created, displayed, and distinguished from one another using different sizes and colors.

Chapter 12:

Having a Good Time with Windows 11

Make the most of your Windows 11 computer by taking full advantage of all of its games, apps, and media capabilities.

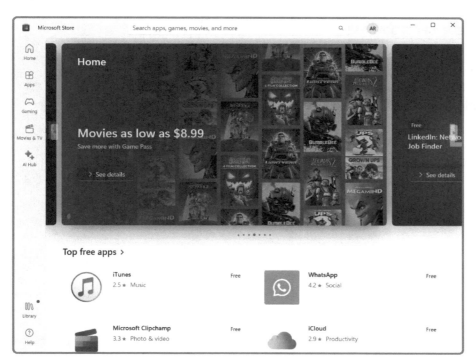

What games am I able to play?

Nearly all of the games that worked with Windows 10's predecessor will work with the new operating system.

Older games created for Windows 8, Windows 7, or earlier operating systems, however, might no longer function on Windows 11.

Several digital gaming storefronts and downloaders, such as Steam, Origin, the Epic Games Store, and the Microsoft Store, are available on Windows 11.

Native Games

Games have long been a part of Windows operating systems. Hearts, Solitaire, 3D Pinball, and Minesweeper are some of the games that bring back the most memories.

Since Windows 11 only supports the Solitaire Collection, which includes **Classic Solitaire, Spider Solitaire, and FreeCell,** the majority of these games are no longer accessible. All of these card games follow the same rules as their analogous real-world counterparts.

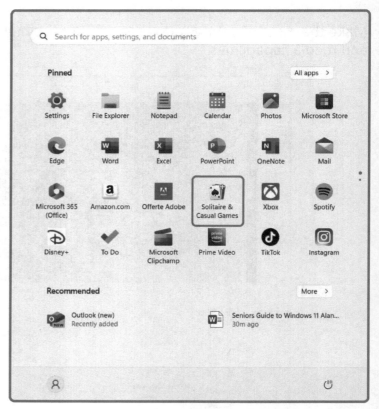

To download and install the Solitaire Collection, open the Microsoft Store by clicking the app icon in your app list or typing its name into the Start menu. Find the Solitaire Collection, then choose Install. By clicking the Play button, the game can be started.

Once the game has started, you can increase its accessibility by pinning it to the Start menu or taskbar. In the taskbar, right-click the game icon and select "Pin to taskbar" or "Pin to Start."

Discover Microsoft Store

You can get all the apps and games you need from the Microsoft App Store. It is the safest way to get content onto your PC, since you won't risk getting viruses or other harmful software on your computer like you might if you download content from an internet browser.

Change the settings for your Microsoft Store account

Your Account

To use the Microsoft Store, you'll need to log in with your Microsoft Account.

Click on your profile picture to the right of the search bar to see these settings. Click "Manage your account and devices." Here, you can see all of your apps, devices, and accounts. You can also see your subscriptions, cancel or renew them, and unlink any devices.

Make Payments

Find and change your payment information by clicking on your profile picture to the right of the search bar and selecting "Payment methods." Here is where you can add your debit card, credit card, bank account, PayPal account, or mobile phone as a payment method for the Microsoft Store.

When you buy a game or app, you can choose any of these ways to pay, and the Microsoft Store will make sure that your money is transferred safely and securely. In this section, you can also see all of the transactions you have made in the past.

How to Redeem Codes

To redeem a gift card or coupon code at the Microsoft Store, simply click on your profile picture found to the right of the search bar and choose "Redeem code or gift cards." You can buy any app, game, or other items from the Microsoft Store using these gift cards.

They can be bought both online and offline, including directly from the Microsoft Store. These cards either reduce the price or provide you with store credits.

Upon purchasing a gift card, you'll get a 25-digit code which you'll need to input in the specified area. The process is the same for promo codes. When making a purchase, you'll have the option to use your gift card, promo code, or another payment method at checkout.

App Settings

Click on your profile picture, situated to the left of the search bar, **to access the app settings.** From there, you can opt to update the app, register, activate offline features, and set videos to play automatically.

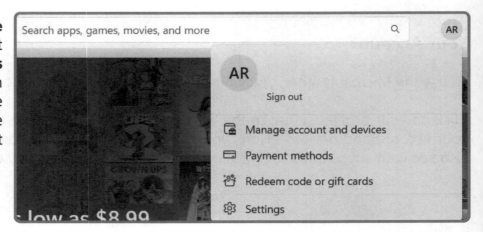

Explore Microsoft Store

When you open the Microsoft Store app, the home screen will show you some of the most popular games and apps that you can buy and download. At the top of the window is a search bar, and on the left is a navigation bar with buttons:

• **Home:** When you land on the main page of the store, it's like walking into a showcase. Featured apps, games, and curated collections are laid out just for you.

• **Apps:** Ever wonder where to find the coolest or top-rated apps? Look no further. This section's got apps for pretty much anything you can dream up.

• **Gaming:** Whether you're into arcade classics, brain-teasing puzzles, epic adventures, or simulations, this is your gaming paradise. From freebies to those worth every penny, and hey, if you've got an Xbox Game Pass, there's stuff here for you too.

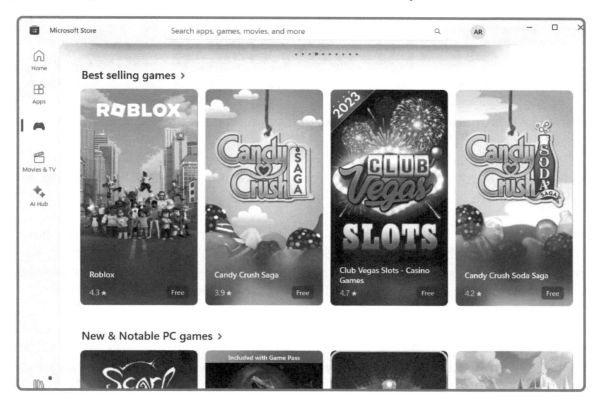

• **Movies & TV:** Think of it as your personal gateway to binge-town. Dive into Netflix, Amazon Prime, Disney+, Hulu, and many others. Looking for a specific show or film? The Microsoft Store will point you to where you can stream it.

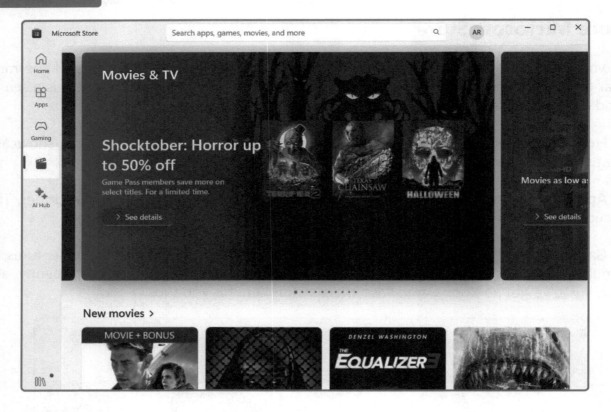

- **Library:** All your downloads, be it apps, games, movies, or that TV series everyone's talking about, are tucked safely here.

- **Help:** Stuck? Lost? Or just got a question? This is your go-to spot for any help navigating the Microsoft Store.

If you're on the hunt for a new game, you've got a couple of options. You can either punch in the game's name in the search bar or let the Microsoft Store throw a few suggestions your way for some fresh fun. They've got a knack for suggesting stuff based on what you've played before. And if you're feeling adventurous, go ahead and explore games by category or genre.

Spotted a game that piques your interest? Click on it! You'll land on its page, packed with descriptions, player ratings, and some honest-to-goodness reviews. And while some games might have a price tag, others won't cost you a dime. To dive into a new gaming experience, either hit the 'Get' button or tap on the price. Don't sweat the techy part - the Microsoft Store's got your back and will set everything up. Once done, 'Launch' lights up, and you're off to the gaming races!

Search on the Store

Ever tried searching for something specific and felt overwhelmed? Well, when you pop a keyword into the Microsoft Store's search bar and hit Enter, you can pick where you want your hunt to focus: be it **'All departments', 'Apps', 'Games', 'Movies', or even 'TV Shows'.** And if you're feeling particularly picky, there's a nifty 'Filters' button on the left. Want games for a certain age group? Or maybe just the free ones? Just tweak the filters to your heart's content.

Managing Your Library

Now, if you're the sort who loses track of all the digital goodies you've snagged, the 'Library' tab is your best pal. It's like a digital bookshelf of everything you've downloaded on your PC. Still waiting on a download or an update? It's there. Got an app on another device but craving it on your current one? A little cloud icon's got you covered. Give it a click, and voila! The app or game lands on your current device, carrying all its data. So, if you were conquering levels on your phone game and fancy doing the same on your PC, everything's right where you left off.

And if you're the kind who likes their apps fresh and updated, the **'Get updates'** button in the Library's top right corner is a magic wand. Give it a click, and the store ensures all your apps and games are in tip-top shape, updating them in the background.

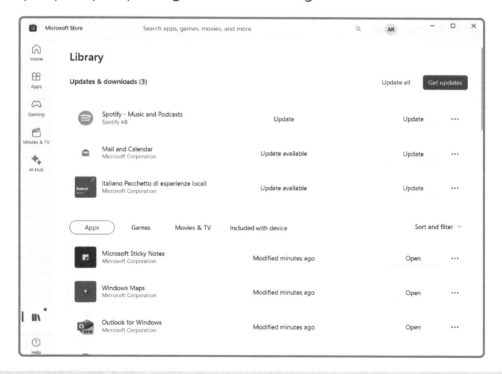

How to Uninstall an App or Game

You can remove and uninstall any app or game from your Windows 11 device using one of two methods.

1) The first way is to use the Start menu:

- To uninstall an app, follow these steps: **open the Start menu, click "All Apps"** in the top right corner, scroll down the list to **find the app you want to get rid of, then right-click it and choose "Uninstall."**

- This method will work for the majority of apps, but some may require additional steps: Confirm your choice by clicking 'Uninstall' in the pop-up window

- Clicking 'Uninstall' on some apps, such as VLC, will **open up the Control Panel to the "Programs and Features" section.**

  o You'll see a list of programs; select the program you want to uninstall once more from the list.

  o Then select the 'Uninstall' button, which is located at the top of the list.

  o You can uninstall any game or program on your computer using this Control Panel method as well.

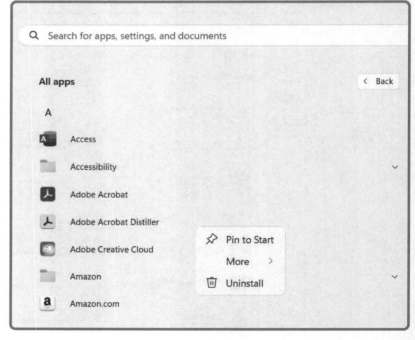

2) Another method for uninstalling an app or game is to go to **Settings**:

- **Open the Settings app**

- **Navigate to Apps > Installed Apps**

- **Find the app you want to remove from the list**

- **Click on the three dots on the right side of the app's name**

- **Select 'Uninstall'**

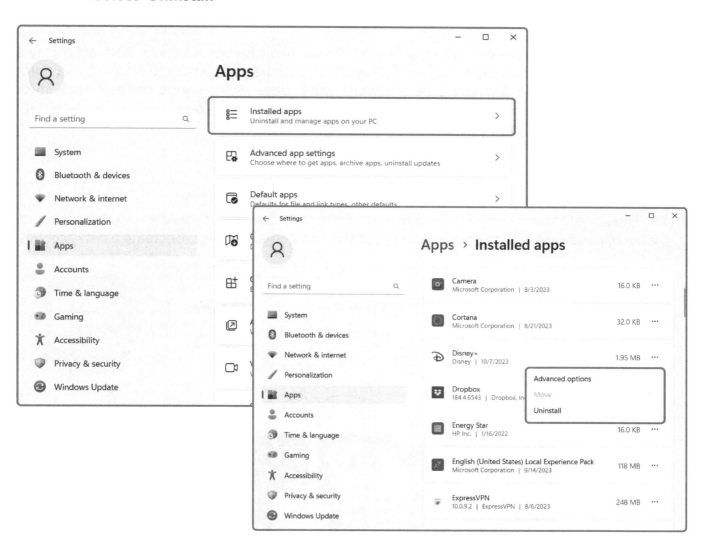

How to Listen to Music or Watch Videos

On a Windows 11 computer, there's no shortage of ways to groove to your favorite tunes. Whether you're kicking it old-school with CDs or MP3s or riding the streaming wave with services like Spotify, just pop open a media player and let the beats drop.

Music Streaming

Groove Music or Windows Media Player

Windows 11's got a couple of built-in gems for all you music lovers out there. Both apps play a good chunk of media files and let you craft playlists to your heart's content. Just give 'em a quick search in the Start menu. But here's the cool part: with Groove Music, your tunes aren't just stuck on one device. Install it on your other gadgets, and like magic, your songs and playlists are right there, ready for on-the-go jam sessions.

Spotify

- The Spotify app is available for download from the Microsoft Store. After installing the app, launch it and sign in with your existing password and email address, or create a new account.

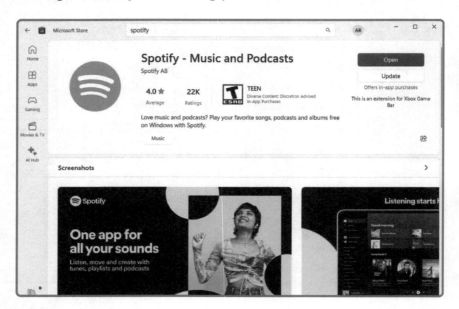

- You can use multiple devices to sign into the same Spotify account, allowing you to take your music and playlists with you wherever you go.

- Use the buttons on the left side to navigate the Spotify app:

  ○ **Browse:** On the hunt for fresh beats or a new artist? This is your starting point. With Radio, let Spotify whip up a tailored playlist from a song, album, or artist you're vibing to.

  ○ **Your Music:** Here's a recap of all the tunes you've been jamming to lately. It includes everything: tracks, albums, your fave artists, and stations. Got some tracks saved offline? They're snug under 'Local files'.

  ○ **Playlists:** Peek here for your music compilations and Spotify's very own playlist picks.

  ○ **Smack dab** in the app's center, get lost exploring new tracks or play your go-to hits. And if you've got a specific tune or artist in mind, that search bar up top? That's your golden ticket.

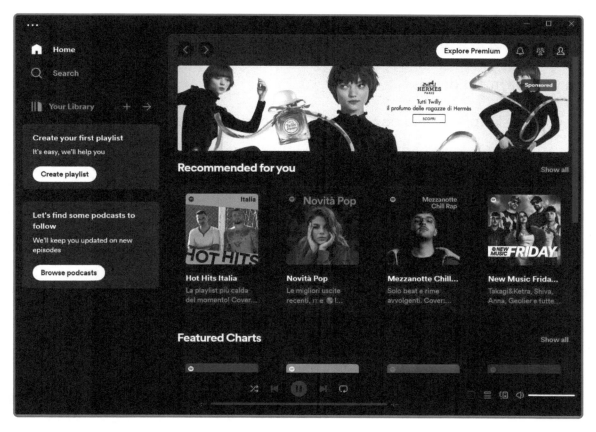

o   Your very own **DJ booth** is at the app's bottom. Play, pause, skip, adjust the volume, or tinker with the settings – all from here.

o   Got friends with killer music taste? Add 'em and see what they're jamming to on the app's right side. Fancy sharing a tune? Shoot it over to them.

Spotify Premium

With the free version of Spotify, you can listen to all of the music and podcasts in the library, but you may be interrupted by ads often. With the free version, you also can't save content to listen to later.

Follow these steps to sign up for Spotify Premium so you can use all of the app's features:

1. Go to **www.spotify.com** and sign in with your email address or username and password.

2. Choose "Upgrade" from the menu.

3. Choose what kind of membership you want and how much you want to pay for it.

4. Type in your payment details

5. Reload your desktop app, and now you can use Spotify Premium.

VLC Media

VLC represents a renowned third-party media player, capable of supporting a vast array of media formats, ranging from videos to music tracks, podcasts, and beyond.

Its interface is designed for clarity and ease of use. To utilize VLC for media playback, one simply locates the desired content within the File Explorer and subsequently drags it into the active VLC application window.

Chapter 13:

Taking Photographs and Other Activities

In Windows 11, snapping a quick photo or shooting a video has never been easier, thanks to Microsoft's integrated tools.

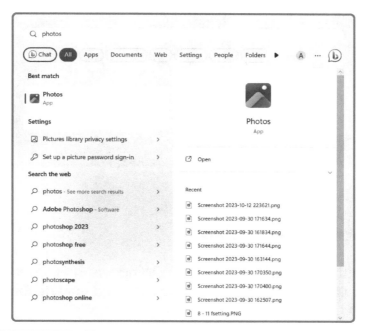

Taking Photos and Videos

If you are using a Windows 11 laptop or mobile device like a tablet, it will likely come with a built-in camera that you can use to take pictures or videos.

- Head over to the Start menu and type in **'Camera'** to see if your device comes with one. If you see an icon, you're good to go!

- Click on that icon to get the Camera app rolling.

- Before diving in, make sure your camera's aimed just right. Use the image preview as a guide to ensure your shot's centered and looks good.

- Feeling ready? Press the **'Capture' button** down on the bottom left to snap a pic.

- Want to shift to video mode? Simply tap the **Video icon** in the Camera app.

- Press **'Record' to start capturing the moment,** and hit it again when you're done to stop the recording. Voilà!

Capture Photo

Record a Video

Viewing Your Photos and Videos

All content captured with your built-in camera in Windows 11 is saved to the **"Camera Roll" folder** in your **Pictures Library**. This media can be accessed **via File Explorer**.

Making Use of the Photos App

Photo Import from Your Camera

Images and videos from a camera, smartphone, or tablet can be imported into Windows 11 computers for storage, viewing, and editing.

- Begin by connecting your camera, smartphone, or tablet to your computer using the USB cable that came with your device.

- If you did everything correctly, you should see a small USB icon in your system tray on the right side of your taskbar.

- Select the Photos app from the Apps list or type 'Photos' into the Start menu to launch it.

- Select **'Import'** from the top right of the Photos app window.

- Select **"Import from a device."**

- You may see a message that says, "Something went wrong at this stage." Make sure your camera/tablet/smartphone is turned on and unlocked. Then choose "Try again."

- The Photos app will launch and begin "looking for new photos and videos." Allow a few minutes to complete this task.

- Choose which photos and videos to import and where you want them saved when the process is finished.

  o   You can change the destination folder or make a new one.

  o   You can import all of your media or just the media you've captured since the last time you imported. You can also use the checkboxes to manually select which photos and videos to import.

  o   Click the Import button, which should display the number of files that will be transferred to your computer.

  o   To complete this process, click OK.

  o   Your photos and videos can now be found in the file you selected.

Image Editing

Want to give your photos a fresh touch? Dive into the Photos app and unleash your creativity.

- Look for the **"Edit image"** button on the toolbar and give it a click.

- Here's the fun part: a toolbar pops up, and it's packed with options.

- Fancy a resize or a change in framing? The Crop tool's got your back.

- Need some tweaks on brightness, contrast, or annoyed by those red eyes? Dive into the Adjustment tool.

- Feeling artsy? The filter tool lets you play with hues and colors till you get just the right vibe.

- Want to add a personal touch or a quick note? Grab the Markup tool to doodle, write, or whatever your heart desires.

- All done? Hit "Save as copy" to keep your masterpiece separate. Or, if you're super confident, drop down the menu and hit "Save" to replace the original with your enhanced version. Go you!

View Photo Details

Within the Photos application, users are afforded the capability to access pivotal data concerning both photographs and videos. This encompasses dimensions, capture date, file architecture, pertinent device specifications, and, where relevant, geographical metadata.

- Firstly, identify and select the particular photograph or video you wish to scrutinize.

- Navigate to, and activate, the Information symbol, characterized by the "i" insignia, situated in the toolbar at the window's zenith.

- Subsequent to this action, a comprehensive information panel dedicated to the selected image or video will materialize on the right-hand side of the interface.

How to Print your Photos

Should one possess a printer equipped with the requisite capabilities, it becomes feasible to produce full-color images on an array of paper types, inclusive of the glossy photographic variety. Prior to initiating this process, it is imperative to ascertain that the printer is both activated and appropriately interfaced.

Using the Photos App

- Open the Photos app and select the image you want to print.

- In the toolbar, click the three-dot button.

- From the drop-down menu, choose Print.

- Choose your printer settings, such as which printer to use, how many copies to make, image quality and resolution, and how the image should be laid out and scaled with the page.

- To send your images to the printer, select Print.

Using File Explorer

- In File Explorer, locate the image you want to print.

- Right-click and choose Print.

- In the Print Dialogue, choose the appropriate printer, paper size, image quality, color, and layout options.

- To send the image to the printer, select Print.

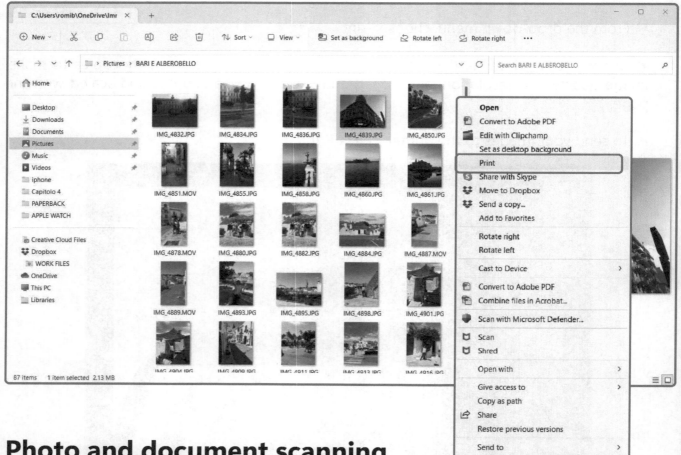

Photo and document scanning

If your printer can copy documents, it can also scan them and save them to your computer.

Scanning App and Scanner

The Windows Scan app is the simplest way to scan a photo or document with a scanner.

1) Download and install the Windows Scan app from the Microsoft Store, then launch it.

2) You will find some printer/scanner options, the file format in which you want your scan saved, the color mode, page size, and the folder in which you want the scan saved:

3) Some printers have feeders and flatbeds; many only have flatbeds. A scanner with a feeder can scan both sides of a page while you need to flip the page over when using a flatbed manually.

4) After you've configured all of these options, click the 'Scan' button at the bottom.

5) The scanner will import your file and save it in the specified location.

Bonus Chapter 14:

Quick Tips and Tricks

Get the most out of your Windows 11 experience by learning some of the most useful tips and tricks.

1) **Increase the size of the text and icons:**

Go to **"Settings"** > **"System"** > **"Display"** to configure your display. Increase the percentage in the "Scale and layout" section to make everything bigger.

2) **Make Use of the Magnifier:**

Type "Magnifier" into the "Start" box. Turn it on and zoom in on specific areas of the screen with your mouse.

3) **Personalize the Taskbar:**

Right-click the taskbar and select "Taskbar settings". You can select which icons to display and where.

4) **Modify Mouse Settings:**

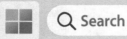 

Go to "Settings" > "Devices" > "Mouse" to configure your mouse. You can adjust the cursor speed and other options here to suit your needs.

5) Make use of the on-screen keyboard:

Type "On-Screen Keyboard" into the "Start" box. This will come in handy if you have trouble typing or if your device has a touchscreen.

6) Make Desktop Shortcuts:

Locate an app or a file, right-click it, and choose **"Send to" > "Desktop (create shortcut)"**.

7) Enable Night Mode:

Go to **"Settings" > "System" > "Display" and enable "Night mode"** to reduce eye strain in the evening.

8) Make Use of Voice Search:

In the Windows search bar, click the **microphone icon** and say what you're looking for.

9) Personalize Your Start Menu:

To pin, unpin, or resize icons in the Start menu, right-click on them.

10) For automatic updates, use "Scheduled Tasks":

Go to **"Settings" > "Update & Security" > "Advanced options"** and select **"Schedule the installation of updates"** to choose when you want updates to be installed.

11) Use "Reminders & Tasks" to Set Reminders:

Type "Reminders" into the "Start" box. You can set reminders and tasks with specific dates and times in this section.

12) Personalize Notifications:

Go to **"Settings" > "System" > "Notifications & actions"** to customize which notifications you receive and how they appear.

13) Protect Your Data with "Windows Backup":

Set up automatic backups by going to **"Settings"** > **"Update & Security"** > **"Backup"** and following the instructions.

14) Modify the Power Saving Settings:

Go to **"Settings"** > **"System"** > **"Power & sleep"** to control how and when your computer enters power-saving mode.

15) Discover Keyboard Shortcuts:

The **desktop is displayed by pressing Windows + D.** The search bar is activated by pressing **Windows + S. Windows + Tab shows you all of your open windows.** These are just a few of the numerous useful shortcuts included with Windows 11.

Bonus Chapter 15:

Common FAQ

1) How can one locate and access files in Windows 11?

Windows 11's File Explorer underwent a redesign for enhanced navigation. To retrieve and access your files:

• Click on the magnifying glass icon in the taskbar or utilize the combination of the Windows key + S.

• Enter the name of your desired file or document.

• As you begin typing, the search results will populate. To access a file, one need only click on it.

Note: Maintaining files within designated folders facilitates swifter navigation.

2) How might one augment the text and icon dimensions for better clarity?

Windows 11 places considerable emphasis on user accessibility:

- To access Settings, click on the gear emblem within the Start menu.

- Opt for "System," subsequently selecting "Display."

- Within this domain, there exists the option to modify the scale of text, applications, and additional items to enhance visibility.

3) Is voice-based typing an available alternative to keyboard input?

Indeed! Windows 11 incorporates a voice-typing feature:

- Activate voice typing by pressing Windows + H.

- With clear articulation, Windows will transcribe your spoken words into text.

- This tool proves invaluable, particularly when composing emails or documents.

4) What methods exist to manage multiple windows on the desktop?

Windows 11 heralds the advent of 'Snap Layouts':

- Hover over the maximize button of an open window.

- A layout selector will manifest. Opt for one that best serves your needs.

- The window will adjust to your selection, enabling the addition of another program in the remaining space.

5) In the event of an inadvertent file deletion, what recourse exists?

There's no cause for undue concern:

- Initiate File Explorer.

 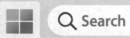 

- Within the left column, opt for "Recycle Bin."

- Identify and right-click on the mistakenly deleted file, selecting "Restore."

- The file will revert to its original position.

6) How might one establish reminders or alarms?

The integral "Alarms & Clock" application is at your service:

- Input "Alarms & Clock" in the search realm.

- To institute a new alarm or reminder, access the 'Alarms' segment and click on the '+' emblem.

- This ensures you remain abreast of essential appointments and events.

7) Can Windows 11's appearance be regressed to mirror its predecessor?

Indeed, it can:

- Execute a right-click in an unoccupied desktop area.

- Opt for "Personalize."

- Within "Start," the Start menu can be realigned to the left, reminiscent of Windows 10.

8) How does one avert the installation of potentially malicious applications?

For a secure experience, utilize the Microsoft Store:

- On the taskbar, click on the designated Microsoft Store emblem.

- This platform allows for safe app searches and installations, given the comprehensive security verification of all offerings.

9)   **In instances where my PC remains silent, what steps should be undertaken?**

To address audio anomalies:

- In the screen's bottom-right corner, click the speaker symbol.

- Ensure the volume isn't set to its minimal position.

- If issues persist, right-click the speaker symbol and select "Troubleshoot sound problems."

10) **What avenues exist to video chat with family members?**

Windows 11 integrates Microsoft Teams natively:

- On the taskbar, select the Teams emblem.

- Sign in or create a new account.

- Once inside, video calls can be initiated by selecting the video camera symbol and extending invitations to family.

- Microsoft Teams simplifies maintaining connections.

Conclusion

Windows 11 is intended to be simple to use, with an intuitive organization system and an appealing design. Even a casual user will benefit from learning some tips and tricks to make their experience faster and smoother.

This title has covered many of the essentials required to work and play confidently on a Windows 11 device. You can see how Windows has evolved and how some of the most recent features have significantly expanded and transformed how people use computers. You should be able to identify the hardware requirements for running the operating system and initiate the upgrade process when new devices become available.

Understanding File Explorer is one of the first and most important steps toward becoming a Windows 11 expert. You should now be able to navigate and find your content, manage, organize, and delete files, as well as curate your libraries to meet your specific requirements. You can also be confident that you can fully utilize the Setting app, including managing your Microsoft account, signing in options, customizing the taskbar, pinning apps, changing your scaling and resolution options, utilizing the various accessibility features, and customizing the appearance of your operating system to suit your personality. You should also be able to add any device, such as a scanner, Bluetooth device, or extra monitor.

The Windows Desktop is where you'll find all of your apps, programs, and windows. You can change the wallpaper on your desktop, rearrange icons and shortcuts, and even create virtual desktops. Moving and resizing windows is as simple as clicking and dragging, and with the addition of widgets in Windows 11, you can display all the information you need to see without cluttering your screen.

Installing new software in Windows 11 is much easier than in previous versions. Use the Microsoft Store to get access to almost any app you can imagine, and your internet browser to find even more content. To reduce the risk of infecting your PC with viruses or malware, only install verified and reviewed products and find good antivirus software.

You can keep up with what's going on in the world around you by using web browsers like Google Chrome or Microsoft Edge. From breaking news to social media and entertainment services such as YouTube. You will be able to save all of your important web pages as bookmarks and use the tab system like a pro.

CONCLUSION

Send a surprise email to your friends and family just because you can! Create an exciting email with the Windows 11 Mail app and attach photos so that your contacts can see what you've been up to lately.

Emojis and animated GIFs can also be included in your emails. Send out invitations to upcoming events using the Mail and Calendar apps, or schedule a video call so that everyone can chat in real time.

Microsoft Teams can make video calls more convenient, efficient, and meaningful. Connect with people all over the world and record your conversations so you can look back and reminisce in the future.

You can also use Teams with confidence to conduct work meetings, interviews, and even give presentations without leaving your house.

Remember to use some productivity apps to make your day-to-day life easier. To-Do lists, calendars, and maps are all available. Make lists to keep track of all your tasks, set deadlines, and plan your trips with real-time traffic data to ensure you are always on time.

To transform your media library, use the newly updated Photos app. Your photos can be sorted, organized, and even edited. Create slideshows and collections to keep your memories close at hand. The Photos app can also record and edit professional-quality videos, which you can then send to others via the Mail app.

Windows 11 has also advanced to the next level of gaming. Explore the vast array of arcade, adventure, puzzle, shooter, and role-playing games available through the Microsoft Store and various game launchers.

Finally, you can impress your kids and grandchildren with your knowledge of Windows shortcuts, hidden menus, customized sound settings, and troubleshooting skills. You will never have to call them again to solve a problem.

Index

INDEX

 Search

INDEX

T

U

V

W

Z